Contents

Contents

Punchouts

Name _____

Strategy Workshop

As you listen to the story "The Sandwich," by
Stephen Krensky, you will stop from time to time
to do some activities on these practice pages.
These activities will help you think about different
strategies that can help you read better. After
completing each activity, you will discuss what
you've written with your classmates and talk
about how to use these strategies.

Remember, strategies can help you become a
better reader. Good readers

- use strategies whenever they read

- use different strategies before, during, and
  after reading

- think about how strategies will help them

Name _____

Strategy 1: Predict/Infer

Use this strategy before and during reading to help make predictions about what happens next or what you're going to learn.

Here's how to use the Predict/Infer Strategy:

1. Think about the title, the illustrations, and what you have read so far.
2. Tell what you think will happen next—or what you will learn. Thinking about what you already know about the subject may help.
3. Try to figure out things the author does not say directly.

Listen as your teacher begins "The Sandwich." When your teacher stops, complete the activity with a partner.

What do you think might happen in the story?

_____

_____

As you listen to the story, you might want to change your prediction or write a new one here.

_____

_____

Name _____

Strategy 2: Phonics/Decoding

Use this strategy during reading when you come across a word you don't know.

Here's how to use the Phonics/Decoding Strategy:

1. Look carefully at the word.
2. Look for word parts that you know and think about the sounds for the letters.
3. Blend the sounds to read the word.
4. Ask yourself if this is a word you know. Does it make sense in the sentence?
5. If not, ask yourself if there's anything else you can try. Should I look in the dictionary?

Listen to your teacher read. When your teacher stops, use the Phonics/Decoding Strategy.

Now write down the steps you used to decode the word *powder*.

_____

_____

_____

_____

Name _____

Strategy 3: Monitor/Clarify

Use this strategy during reading whenever you're confused about what you are reading.

Here's how to use the Monitor/Clarify Strategy:

- Ask yourself if what you're reading makes sense—or if you are learning what you need to learn.
- If you don't understand something, reread, look at the illustrations, or read ahead.

Listen to your teacher read. When your teacher stops, answer the questions with a partner.

1. What is Lionel's problem?

_____

_____

2. Can you tell from listening to the story what Lionel's problem is? Why or why not?

_____

_____

3. How can you find out what Lionel's problem is if you're confused?

_____

_____

Name _____

Strategy 4: Question

Use this strategy during and after reading to ask questions about important ideas in the story.

Here's how to use the Question Strategy:

- Ask yourself questions about important ideas in the story.
- Ask yourself if you can answer these questions.
- If you can't answer the questions, reread and look for answers in the text. Thinking about what you already know and what you've read in the story may help you.

Listen to your teacher read. Then complete the activity with a partner to ask yourself questions about important ideas in the story.

Think about the story and respond below.

Write a question you might ask yourself at this point in the story.

_____

_____

_____

_____

Name _____

Strategy 5: Evaluate

Use this strategy during and after reading to help you form an opinion about what you read.

Here's how to use the Evaluate Strategy:

- Think about how the author makes the story come alive and makes you want to read it.
- Think about what was entertaining, informative, or useful about the selection.
- Think about how well you understood the selection and whether you enjoyed reading it.

Listen to your teacher read. When your teacher stops, answer the questions with a partner.

1. Do you think this story is entertaining? Why?

_____

_____

2. Is the writing clear and easy to understand?

_____

_____

3. Did the author make the characters interesting and believable?

_____

Name _____

Strategy 6: Summarize

Use this strategy after reading to summarize what you read.

Here's how to use the Summarize Strategy:

- Think about the characters.
- Think about where the story takes place.
- Think about the problem in the story and how the characters solve it.
- Think about what happens in the beginning, middle, and end of the story.

Think about the story you just listened to. Answer the questions with a partner to show that you understand how to identify story parts that will help you summarize the story.

1. Who is the main character?

_____

2. Where does the story take place?

_____

3. What is the problem and how is it resolved?

_____

_____

Name _____

The Sandwich, by Stephen Krensky

Lionel liked peanut butter and jelly sandwiches.
He didn't like jelly and peanut butter sandwiches.

Make a shopping list for your favorite lunch food.

My Lunch List

What is your favorite lunch? Draw a picture of
your lunch in the tray.

Name _____

Choose the letter that completes the
name of each food. Write the letter on
the line at the beginning of each word.

| p | m | w | b | j | s | t | c | l |

___ uice   ___ andwich   ___ opcorn

___ arrot   ___ ilk   ___ anana

___ omato   ___ affles   ___ ettuce

_____

Writing Words You Know

Write a word you know on the line beside each
beginning sound.

d_____   w_____   h_____

f_____   z_____   r_____

Name _____

Circle the letter that stands for the sound you hear at the **end** of each picture name.

d t p

n d l

g p j

r l t

k s d

n b z

l r s

c t b

z m g

Writing Words You Know

Write a word you know on the line beside each ending sound.

_____ p   _____ l   _____ n

_____ t   _____ b   _____ m

Name _____

Look at the pictures. Read the words in the box.
Write the word that names each picture.

stick	truck	drink
flag	clown	smile

_____   _____   _____

_____   _____   _____

Writing Words You Know

Write a word you know on the line beside each
beginning cluster.

br_____   fl_____   st_____

pr_____   gl_____   tr_____

Name _____

Write the letters that stand for the beginning
sounds you hear in each picture name.

br	fl	cl	tr	sn	cr	st

Writing Words You Know

Write a word you know on the line beside
each cluster.

bl_____   fr_____   pl_____

dr_____   st_____   gl_____

Name _____

Write **ch**, **sh**, **th**, or **wh** to finish each picture name.

tee_____   sandwi____   _____ip

_____eat   bea_____   _____irty

_____ick   di_____   clo_____

_____

Writing Words You Know

Write a word you know on the line beside each beginning digraph.

sh_____   ch_____

wh_____   th_____

Name _____

Write **ch**, **sh**, or **th** to complete each picture name. Then draw a line to connect the row of three pictures with the same sound.

pea_____	bu_____	_____umb
_____eep	_____air	pa_____
fi_____	_____orn	_____ain

_____

Writing Words You Know
Write a word you know on the line beside each digraph.

_____ ch _____ sh _____ th

Name _____

Complete each puzzle with the correct vowel. Then use the words to complete the sentences under each picture.

	K	
S	W	M
	N	
	G	

The _____ can

_____ very fast.

	h	
w		t
	n	

The _____ got

very _____.

	r	
b		g
	g	

The _____ hid under

the _____.

	c	
h		t
	t	

The _____ wore a

funny _____.

	d	
h		t
	g	

The sun made the

_____ very _____.

Name _____

Write a letter on a line to build a word that
rhymes with the picture name.

_____ an
_____ an
_____ an

_____ ot
_____ ot
_____ ot

_____ ug
_____ ug
_____ ug

_____ et
_____ et
_____ et

_____ ish
_____ ish
_____ ish

Writing Words You Know

Write a word you know on the line beside the
short vowel sound. The word can have the vowel
sound in it or begin with the short vowel sound.

a_____   e_____   i_____

o_____   u_____

Name _____

Look at the pictures. Read the words in the box.
Write the word that names each picture.

bee	flute	leaf
gate	goat	tie
vine	nail	rope

_____

_____

_____

Writing Words You Know

Write a word you know on the lines with the
long vowel sound.

____ o ____ e   ____ a ____ e   ____ i ____ e

____ ee ____   ____ o ____ e

Name _____

Add an *e* to the end of each group of letters.
Then draw a picture of the word you made.

can _____

kit _____

rop _____

cub _____

tre _____

Writing Words You Know

Write a word you know with the long vowel
sound beside each vowel. The word can begin
with the vowel or have the vowel in it.

a_____   e_____   i_____

o_____   u_____

Name _____

Silly Stories

Write your own silly story. Think of a silly character, such as a plant or animal that speaks, then fill in the blanks to complete the story.

One day, _____

came into our classroom. It _____

and then it _____ .

Finally, my teacher _____ .

Now write three sentences that tell more about what happened. Then draw your silly character in the box.

_____

_____

_____

_____

Name _____

Silly Stories

Fill in the chart as you read the stories.

	Where do the silly stories in this theme take place?	What silly things do some of the characters do?
Dragon Gets By		
Julius		
Mrs. Brown Went to Town		

Name _____

Making Words

When you put these letters together, they make words.

m + a + p = map   p + i + n = pin

**Put these letters together to write words with
the short *a* and short *i* sound.**

1. f + a + n = _____

2. h + i + l + l = _____

3. b + a + t = _____

4. m + i + t + t = _____

5. h + a + t = _____

**Now use the short *a* and short *i* words you wrote
above to complete the sentences below.**

6. The dog ran up the _____ .

7. Martin caught the ball in his _____ .

8. Juan turns on the _____ when he is hot.

9. I wear my _____ on my head.

10. Sue hit the ball with the _____ .

Theme 1: **Silly Stories**   3

Name _____

Shopping for Food

Write the correct word to finish each sentence.

Word Bank

bought	kitchen	roll	front	until

1. Mr. Janson went to the store and

   _____ many kinds of food.

2. He stood in line and paid for his food at the

   _____ of the store.

3. Mr. Janson waited in line _____

   it was his turn.

4. He did not let his cart _____

   away.

5. When he got home, he took the food into the

   _____.

Write a sentence that tells about something that you have bought.

_____

_____

Name _____

Words That Fit

Use words from the box to complete the sentences in the puzzle.

Word Bank

hungry vegetables shopping shoppers dairy balanced

Across

1. If you are buying food at a food store, you are _____ .

2. Carrots, peas, and spinach are _____ .

3. Milk, cheese, and ice cream are _____ products.

5. People who buy food at a food store are called _____ .

Down

4. When you need to eat, you feel _____ .

6. If you eat foods from the basic food groups, you have a _____ diet.

Name _____

Story Map

As you read the story, complete the story map below.

Who (Who is in the story?)

_____

Where (Where does the story take place?)

_____

_____

Beginning (pages 19–22) (What happens?)

_____

_____

Middle (pages 23–32) (What happens?)

_____

_____

End (pages 33–34) (What happens?)

_____

_____

Name _____

Ask Away

Below are questions about the story _Dragon Gets By_.
Write an answer to each question.

1. Why didn't the food that Dragon
   bought at the store fit in his car?

   _____

2. What did Dragon plan to do so he could
   fit the food in his car?

   _____

   _____

3. Why couldn't Dragon fit in his car?

   _____

   _____

4. How did Dragon get his car home?

   _____

   _____

5. How did Dragon feel when he got home?

   _____

   _____

Name _____

Story Structure

**Read the story and then answer the
questions on the next page.**

Raccoon's Party

Raccoon wanted someone to talk to,
but he lived alone. He decided to have
a party. He put up balloons and made
some good food. He invited a few friends
to come to his party. Soon his friends were
ringing the doorbell. Raccoon asked them
into his house. He enjoyed talking to his
friends. It wasn't long before they didn't have
anything else to say to each other. It was too
early for the party to end, so Raccoon invited
more friends to his party.

Lots of Raccoon's friends came to his party.
Everyone was having a great time. That is,
everyone except Raccoon. The house was so
crowded, Raccoon could barely move. The
party was so noisy that Raccoon couldn't
talk to any of his friends. Raccoon knew what
to do. He wiggled his way past everyone to
the front door and stepped out of his house.
He was glad to be outside where he could
finally get some peace and quiet!

Name _____

Story Structure continued

**After you've read the story, answer
each question below.**

Who (Who is in the story?)

1. _____

2. _____

Where (Where does the story take place?)

3. _____

Beginning (What happens?)

4. _____

5. _____

Middle (What happens?)

6. _____

7. _____

8. _____

9. _____

End (What happens?)

10. _____

Name _____

Shopping for Endings

Example:

help + s

helps

help + ed

helped

help + ing

helping

Look at each base word and ending. Put each base word together with an ending to make a new word. Write the new word on the line. Then read the new word.

1. work   + s   + ed

    _____   _____

2. play   + s   + ed

    _____   _____

3. talk   + ed   + ing

    _____   _____

4. eat   + s   + ing

    _____   _____

5. stay   + s   + ing

    _____   _____

Name _____

Apple or Fish?

► Five Spelling Words have the short
  a vowel sound that you hear at the
  beginning of .

► Five Spelling Words have the short
  i vowel sound that you hear in .

► The words **was** and **I** are special.

1. bag
2. win
3. is
4. am
5. his
6. has
7. ran
8. if
9. dig
10. sat
11. was*
12. I*

**Write the Spelling Words with the short *a* vowel
sound under the apple and the short *i* vowel
sound under the fish.**

apple

fish

_____   _____

_____   _____

_____   _____

_____   _____

_____   _____

**Write the two Spelling Words that do not have the
vowel sounds you hear in *apple* or *fish*.**

_____   _____

Theme 1: **Silly Stories**   **11**

Name _____

Spelling Spree

Word Clues Write a Spelling Word that answers each clue.

Spelling Words

1. bag
2. win
3. is
4. am
5. his
6. has
7. ran
8. if
9. dig
10. sat
11. was*
12. I*

1. Something to carry things in _____

2. Something you do with a shovel

   _____

3. A word that can be found in **ham**, **jam**,

   Pam, and **Sam** _____

4. This word has only one letter

   _____

5. Add **h** to the beginning of **as** to

   make this word _____

6. Add **w** to the beginning of **as** to

   make this word _____

7. The word **is** can be found inside

   this word _____

8. A word that rhymes with **cat** and

   rat _____

Name _____

Proofreading and Writing

Proofreading In the letter below, find and circle four Spelling Words that are not spelled correctly. Write each word correctly.

Dear Chris,

I play on a baseball team. Our team name iz the Dragons. My hat has a picture of a dragon on it! I play third base. Iff we win our next two games, we will be in first place. I sat out today's game. My knee wus hurting. I hope I can play next week, and I hope the Dragons wen!

Your friend,

Bob

Spelling Words

1. bag
2. win
3. is
4. am
5. his
6. has
7. ran
8. if
9. dig
10. sat
11. was*
12. I*

1. _____   3. _____

2. _____   4. _____

Write a Letter Write a letter to one of your friends. Tell about something that has happened to you. Write your letter on another sheet of paper. Use Spelling Words from the list.

Name _____

Pairs of Pears

Draw a line from each word on the left to a word on the right that sounds the same but has a different meaning.

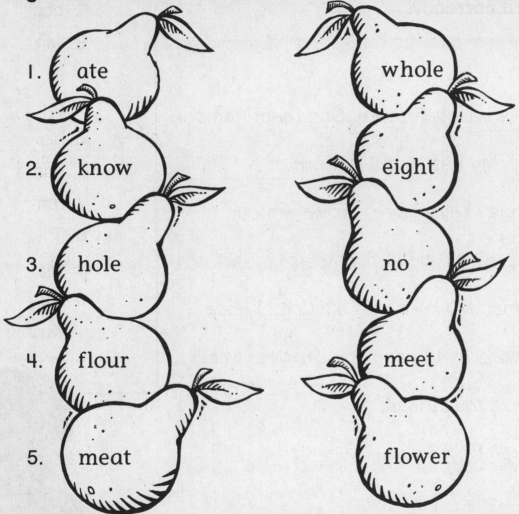

1. ate

2. know

3. hole

4. flour

5. meat

whole

eight

no

meet

flower

Choose one of the pairs of words. Write two sentences.

Use one of the words in each sentence.

_____

_____

_____

Name _____

Dragon Gets By

Grammar Skill What Is a Sentence?

Lightning Sentences

► A sentence tells what someone or something does.

Write *yes* or *no* to tell whether each of these is a sentence.

1. Lightning struck the tree. _____

2. Rain splashes against the window. _____

3. A strong wind. _____

4. Dark clouds fill the sky. _____

5. We heard a loud clap of thunder. _____

6. We could see the lightning. _____

7. Shovels the snow off the sidewalk. _____

8. Snowflakes float to the ground. _____

9. Makes it warm outside. _____

10. The rain caused a flood. _____

Name _____

Follow the Sentence Road

A sentence tells what someone or something does.
**Find the store by coloring only the pieces
of the road that are complete sentences.**

A large fly.

My dog runs fast.

The tiger is in the river.

Live in the ocean.

Pigs in the mud.

The rabbit hops away.

The snake.

The cat is by the fireplace.

STORE

OPEN

Five cows are in the field.

Reach with their necks.

Name _____

Cans of Sentences

Circle the cans with complete sentences.

mom bought
two cans of
soup

places the
cans in the
cupboard

the peaches
in this can
are sweet

there are
eight cans
on the shelf

opened the
can of peas

some kinds
of juice are
sold in cans

cans of
green beans

the labels
tell what is
inside each
can

**Write each sentence you circled. Remember to use
capital letters and periods.**

1. _____

2. _____

3. _____

4. _____

5. _____

Name _____

Who Is Dragon?

Read the questions in the circles. Write your answers in the boxes.

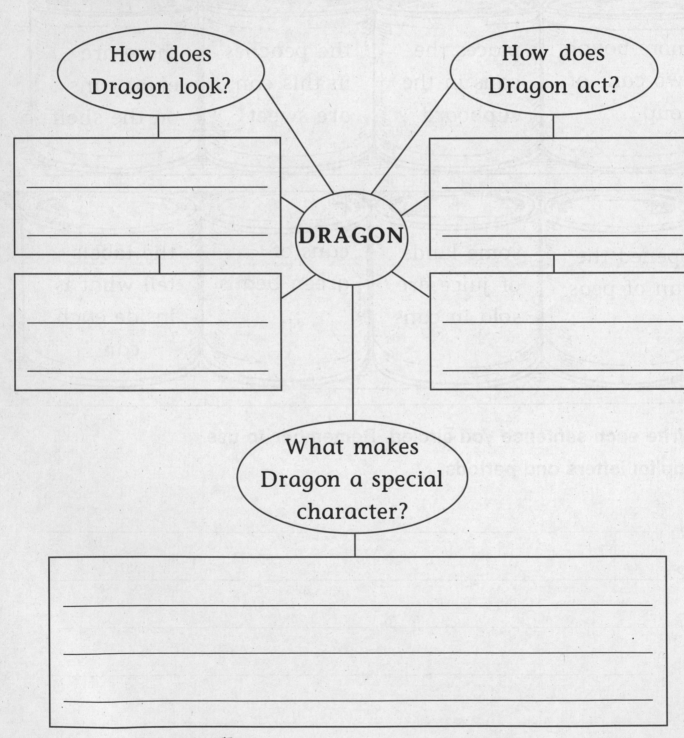

Name _____

Telling More

**Read each sentence. Rewrite the sentences
so they tell more about the characters.**

Example: David likes to write.

David likes to write long silly stories.

1. Jessie has long hair.

_____

_____

2. The horse is wild.

_____

_____

3. The woman is strong.

_____

_____

4. The ape is silly.

_____

_____

5. My dog is a fast runner.

_____

_____

Name _____

Revising Your Story

Put a check next to the sentences that tell about your story.

Superstar

☐ My story has a good beginning.

☐ My story has a middle.

☐ My story has a good ending.

☐ My story has a good title.

☐ I used complete sentences.

Rising Star

☐ My story needs a good beginning.

☐ The middle of my story could be better.

☐ My story needs an ending.

☐ I need to add a good title to my story.

☐ Some of my sentences aren't complete.

Name _____

Writing Sentences

A Funny Clown Read each sentence. Write
the parts of the sentence on the lines.

1. The clown ran around the ring.

   Who or What? _____

   What happened? _____

2. The clown jumped up and down.

   Who or What? _____

   What happened? _____

3. The little dog chased the clown.

   Who or What? _____

   What happened? _____

Write one or two sentences to finish the story.

_____

_____

_____

Theme 1: **Silly Stories**   21

Name _____

Spelling Words

These Spelling Words are words that you use in your writing. Look carefully at how they are spelled. Write the missing letters in the Spelling Words below. Use the words in the box.

1. w____s

2. m____

3. s_____d

4. th_____

5. h_____e

6. ____ny

7. th____

8. wi_____

9. i____

10. a____

11. y_____

12. o_____

Spelling Words

1. the
2. will
3. it
4. have
5. as
6. my
7. was
8. you
9. they
10. said
11. off
12. any

Write the Spelling Words below.

_____   _____

_____   _____

_____   _____

_____   _____

Spelling Spree

Use the Spelling Words to complete the sentences. Write the words in the circus tent.

1. He ____ happy to go to the circus.
2. He wanted to see ____ clowns.
3. They ____ be funny.
4. Do ____ think the show will start on time?
5. "Yes, ____ will begin at six o'clock," said Tom.
6. Are there ____ elephants in the show?
7. "No, ____ are coming tomorrow."
8. We will ____ to come back to see them.

Spelling Words
1. the
2. will
3. it
4. have
5. as
6. my
7. was
8. you
9. they
10. said
11. off
12. any

1. _____ 5. _____

2. _____ 6. _____

3. _____ 7. _____

4. _____ 8. _____

Write the Spelling Words that rhyme with *sky* and *jazz*.

9. _____   10. _____

Theme 1: **Silly Stories** 23

Name _____

Proofreading and Writing

Proofreading Find and circle misspelled Spelling Words in this story. Then write each word correctly.

Spelling Words

1. the
2. will
3. it
4. have
5. as
6. my
7. was
8. you
9. they
10. said
11. off
12. any

Holly wuz the Walls's funny little kitten.   Thay liked to watch her get up on her hind legs and dance around. One day she hopped into an open bureau drawer and fell asleep.

Brianna Wall came into the room. "I haf to get my new shorts," she sed.   She opened the drawer and Holly jumped up. Brianna was surprised! Then the drawer fell. The clothes landed on the floor. Holly ran of!

1. _____   2. _____   3. _____

4. _____   5. _____

✏ **Write Funny Sentences** Write sentences about funny things or something that happens that is funny. Use as many Spelling Words as you can in your sentences.

This Little Piggy

**Write each word from the box under the pig
that has the same vowel sound.**

Word Bank

| hog | pet | mud | pen | grunt | hot |

bed

box

cup

_____

_____

_____

_____

_____

_____

Finish the sentences below. Use the words you just wrote.

1. Pigs live in a _____ near the barn.

2. They make a noise that sounds like a _____.

3. Sometimes pigs get _____ in the sun.

4. They lie in _____ to stay cool.

5. A pig can also be called a _____.

6. Some people have a pig for a _____.

Theme 1: **Silly Stories**   25

Name _____

Pick a Pet

Write a word from the box to complete each sentence.

Word Bank

brought	reason	special	surprise

1. One day Mom _____ home a kitten.

2. It was a big _____ to everyone in the family.

3. The _____ Mom got the kitten was that she wanted a pet.

4. She thought the kitten was _____ because it had blue eyes.

What kind of pet would you like to have? Draw a picture of it. Write a sentence to tell why it would be a special pet.

_____

_____

_____

Name _____

Mind Your Manners

Living with other people can be difficult. Here are some rules to help everyone get along. Use the vocabulary words to complete the sentences.

Vocabulary

crumbs

slurped

imitation

spread

noise

1. Use a broom to sweep up cookie

   _____ on the floor.

2. Turn the radio low to keep the

   _____ down.

3. Keep your toys in one place so they are

   not _____ out.

4. After you have _____
   a drink, say "Excuse me!"

5. If you act like an animal, do the

   _____ outside.

Think about the rules at home. Write one of the rules on the lines.

_____

_____

Name _____

Fantasy and Realism Chart

Use the chart below to help you keep track of things that could really happen and things that could not.

Could Really Happen	Could Not Really Happen

Name _____

Hidden Message

Use the clues to complete the puzzle.

1. Julius made big _____ .
2. Julius and Maya went to the store to try on _____ , hats, and shoes.
3. They loved to _____ to jazz records.
4. Julius loved to eat peanut butter from a _____ .
5. Mom and Dad said Julius made too much _____ .
6. Maya taught Julius good _____ .
7. Maya and Julius liked to _____ at the playground.

1. ___ ___ ___ ___ ___ ___ □

2.   ___ ___ ___ ___ □ ___

3.   ___ ___ □ ___ ___ ___

4.   ___ ___ ___ □ ___ ___

5.   ___ ___ ___ ___ □ ___

6.   ___ ___ ___ ___ ___ □ ___ ___

7.   ___ ___ ___ ___ □

Write the letters from the boxes to find out what Maya and Julius taught each other.

□ □ □ □ □ □ □

Name _____

Fantasy and Realism

Read the story below and then answer the questions on the next page.

A Picnic in the Park

It was such a nice day, Gloria decided to go to the park. She packed a picnic. Then she called her dog, Ben.

"Let's go to the park, Ben. I packed a picnic for us." Ben came running. He stopped in front of Gloria. Ben gave her a big dog lick.

"I love the park," Ben said. "What did you pack for me to eat?"

"I packed your favorite dog food and some bones," answered Gloria.

"This is going to be a great day!" said Ben. He put on his sunglasses. "I can hardly wait to go down the slide. And I'll push you on the swing."

Ben ran to get some things he wanted to take to the park. He got his swim fins and a big towel. He got his best ball and a good book to read.

"Ben, you don't need all that stuff!" Gloria said. "Yes I do!" Ben answered.

"Okay, but you forgot the most important thing," Gloria said.

"My leash! I'll get it!" cried Ben.

Name _____

Fantasy and Realism continued

Answer the questions. Use complete sentences.

1. Which character could be real?

_____

2. Which character does make-believe things?

_____

3. Name three things in the story that are make-believe.

_____

_____

_____

4. Name three things in the story that are real.

_____

_____

What do you think Gloria and Ben will do at the park? On another sheet of paper, write an ending for the story.

Name _____

Pet Show

**Mrs. Johnson's class had a show-and-tell about pets.
Read the rhymes to find out about the animals at the
show. Write words from the box to complete the rhymes.**

Word Bank

ants   cat   rabbit   fish   pig

1. Dan's pet would purr when he gave it a pat.

   He brought to school a little black _____.

2. Jill's pet has a tail and fins that swish.

   She showed the class a tank with a _____.

3. Jack's pet hopped away before he could grab it.

   He spent the whole time chasing his _____.

4. One of Sal's pets crawled up his pants,

   After he showed the class his farm of _____.

5. Jim's pet likes to lie in mud and likes to dig.

   The pet he brought was a big pink _____.

32   Theme 1: **Silly Stories**

Name _____

What's the Sound?

▶ The vowel sound in **job** and **pop** is called
the short **o** sound. The short **o** sound
may be spelled **o**. The words **from** and
of are special. The vowel **o** does not
spell the short **o** sound.

▶ The vowel sound in **pet** and **leg** is called
the short **e** sound. The word **any** is
special. The short **e** sound is not spelled
with the vowel **e**.

▶ The vowel sound in **nut** and **rug** is
called the short **u** sound.

**Write each Spelling Word under the pet with the
matching vowel sound.**

Spelling Words

1. fox
2. wet
3. nut
4. job
5. leg
6. fun
7. went
8. mop
9. hug
10. from*
11. any*
12. of *

short o   short u

short e

_____   _____   _____

_____   _____   _____

_____   _____   _____

Now write the 3 words with the * beside them.

_____   _____   _____

Theme 1: **Silly Stories**   33

Spelling Spree

Word Groups **Think about the meaning of each group of words. Write the Spelling Word that goes with each group.**

1. broom, rake, _____

2. bear, wolf, _____

3. arm, foot, _____

4. all, some, _____

5. bean, grape, _____

6. work, office, _____

7. gone, left, _____

8. hold, squeeze, _____

Write a sentence using one of the Spelling Words that didn't go with any of the groups.

9. _____

_____

Proofreading and Writing

Proofreading **Circle four Spelling Words that are wrong in this letter.**

Dear Grandmother,

      I have a new dog. His name is Josh.

He is funn to play with. Josh likes to run

frm one side of the yard to the other.

Sometimes it is a big job to take care uf

Josh. He likes to sit in his water dish. He

gets all weet. Then he shakes himself.

      Love,

      Rita

Spelling Words

1. fox
2. wet
3. nut
4. job
5. leg
6. fun
7. went
8. mop
9. hug
10. from*
11. any*
12. of *

Write each word you circled. Spell the word correctly.

1. _____   2. _____

3. _____   4. _____

Write an Explanation Think of all the care a pet needs. On a separate sheet of paper, write what you would do to take care of a pet. Use Spelling Words from the list.

Name _____

Means the Same

Word Bank

hat	ship	bag	plate	wash	start

In each ball, write a word from the box that means the same or almost the same as the word in the ball.

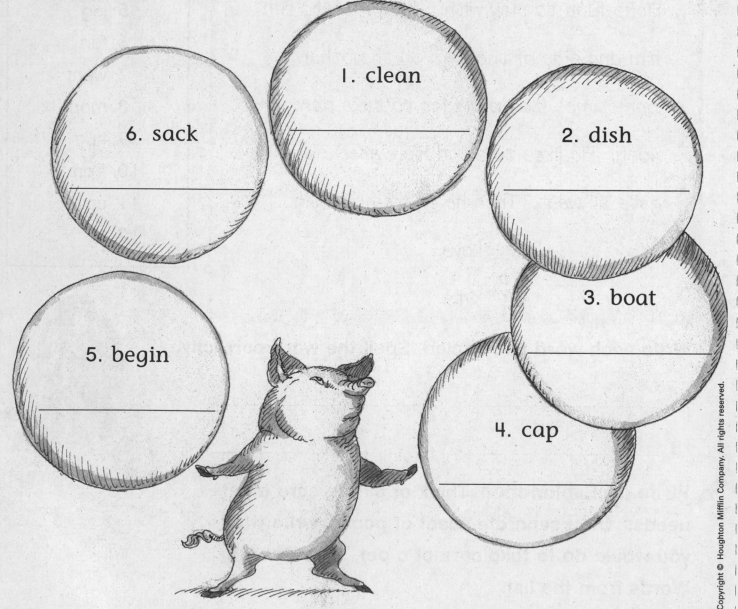

6. sack _____

1. clean _____

2. dish _____

3. boat _____

5. begin _____

4. cap _____

Name _____

Who or What?

► A sentence is a group of words that tells what
someone or something did or does.

► The naming part of a sentence tells whom or
what the sentence is about.

Word Bank

| milk | floor | mop | fox | cup |

**Look at the picture. Then read each sentence.
Write the naming part to complete the sentence.**

1. A _____ fell off the table.

2. The _____ spilled out.

3. The _____ has to clean
up the mess.

4. A _____ will soak up the milk.

5. Then the _____ will be clean
again.

Name _____

Animal Manners

Word Bank

| fly | fox | bear | bees | kangaroo |

Write the naming word from the box that rhymes with the word in dark print in the sentences below.

1. These _____ say **please** when they ask for something.

2. A _____ asks what a guest would like to **do**.

3. The _____ says **good-bye** before hanging up the phone.

4. A _____ likes to **share** toys.

5. That _____ picks up his **socks**.

Name _____

You're Last

Rewrite each of the sentences. Name yourself last.

1. I and Casey went swimming.

   _____

2. I and my friend are going to the movies.

   _____

3. I and my mother ate lunch at school.

   _____

Draw a picture of you and your friend doing something.
Write a sentence to go with your picture.

Name _____

Getting Ready to Respond

**Use the chart to help you write a response journal entry
about the story _Julius_.**

What is the date?

_____

What is the title of the story?

_____

Who is the main character?

_____

What do you like best about the story?

_____

_____

Would you tell a friend to read the story?

_____

What example from the story explains why you like it?

_____

_____

Name _____

Date It!

Rewrite the journal entry on the lines below. Write the circled words correctly.

(3 March 2001)

I read the story (Lost in the park.) The main character in this story was Connor. My favorite part was when he found his mother. I like it because (connor) was brave. Even though he was scared, he didn't cry. I am going to tell a friend to read this story because it is a very good story.

_____

_____

_____

_____

_____

_____

Name _____

Long Vowel Game

**Read the sentences. Draw a circle around each word
that has a long vowel sound and the CVCe pattern.**

1. We would like to play a game with you.

2. You count to five while we look for a place to hide.

3. When you count, you need to face the gate.

4. We can play until it is time to go inside.

**Now write each word you circled under the word that
has the same vowel sound and the CVCe pattern.**

late   **nine**

_____   _____

_____   _____

_____   _____

_____   _____

_____   _____

Name _____ .

Chicken Riddle

Use words from the box to finish the sentences.

Vocabulary

different   floor   letter   move   poor   word

1. When you ___ ___ ___ ___ , you go

       2   13

   to a new place to live.

2. If something is not the same, it is

  ___ ___ ___ ___ ___ ___ ___ ___ ___ .

   12   11   9   1

3. Can you spell the ___ ___ ___ ___ **town**?

                           6

4. My ___ ___ ___ ___ dog hurt his leg.

             8

5. The glass broke when it hit the ___ ___ ___ ___ ___ .

                                             10

6. A ___ ___ ___ ___ ___ ___ is something

        7   4   5   3

   you write to someone.

Write the letters above the numbers to answer this riddle.

Why did the chicken cross the road?

___ ___ g ___ ___ ___ ___ ___ h ___

 1   2   3   4   5   6   1   7

___ ___ h ___ ___ s ___ ___ ___

 8   4   9   10   11   12   13

Name _____

Picture the Vocabulary

Write each word from the box next to its correct definition.

> ## Vocabulary
>
> commotion   released   delivered   tired   feathers   wearing

1. something handed over to someone _____

2. having clothing on the body _____

3. light, soft parts of a bird _____

4. having set something free _____

5. noisy excitement _____

6. having little strength or energy _____

Now use the picture to finish these sentences.

7. As soon as the _____ was

   released, the **commotion** began. First,

   _____

   and then, _____

   and finally, _____

   _____

Name _____

Prediction Chart

As you read the story, complete the chart.

What Happens in the Story

_____

_____

_____

_____

What Would Happen If . . .

_____

_____

_____

_____

Theme 1: **Silly Stories**   45

Name _____

Story Time

Use the phrases in the box to complete the sentences.

> grabbed her feet   Mrs. Brown's house   in the barn out back
> crashed through the floor   to be good   go to the hospital

Saturday: Mrs. Brown rode away on her bicycle. As she went down the road, a dog _____. Mrs. Brown got hurt. She had to _____.

Monday: Mrs. Brown sent a letter. She told the animals _____. But the cow, pigs, ducks, and yak did not listen. They moved into _____.

Tuesday: When Mrs. Brown came home, she went to bed. She did not know that the cow, pigs, ducks, and yak were in her bed. Suddenly, the bed _____. They all went to the hospital. Soon it was time to go home. Now they all live together _____.

Name _____

Predicting Outcomes

Read the story and then complete the chart on the next page.

Pets in a Classroom

Mr. Clark's class was excited today. The children had brought their pets to school. There were three little dogs, one puppy, two cats, two kittens, one parrot, two goldfish, one lizard, one snake, two hamsters, one turtle, one rabbit, and even one chicken. The animals sat quietly while Mr. Clark talked about each of them.

At lunchtime the children left the animals in the classroom. As soon as the door was closed, the animals got into trouble. The dogs chased the cats. The hamsters and turtle ate the children's work. The puppy tried to catch the parrot, and the kittens tried to catch the fish. The rabbit knocked over some paint, and it spilled onto the lizard. The snake crawled into Mr. Clark's desk, and the chicken laid an egg on top of it!

When the class got back from lunch, the children saw the mess. But Mr. Clark did not notice.

Name _____

Predicting Outcomes continued

After you read the story, complete the chart below.

Prediction Chart
What Happens in the Story

1. _____

2. _____

3. _____

4. _____

5. _____

What Would Happen If . . .

_____

_____

_____

_____

_____

_____

Name _____

Vowel Sound Bubbles

Read each word aloud. Listen for the vowel sound.

**Color bubbles that have words with a
short *o* sound yellow.**

**Color bubbles that have words with a
short *u* sound blue.**

**Color bubbles that have words with a
short *e* sound green.**

went

upstairs

ducks

frog

just

ten

tested

dropped

hospital

butter

Theme 1: **Silly Stories**   **49**

Name _____

Sorting Spelling Words

Ten Spelling Words have a long vowel sound spelled with the CVCe pattern. The words **give** and **have** do not follow this rule. They have the CVCe pattern, but they do not have long vowel sounds.

Write each word in the box under the word with the same vowel sound.

bike

1. _____
2. _____
3. _____
4. _____
5. _____
6. _____

gate

7. _____
8. _____
9. _____
10. _____

Write the Spelling Word that answers each question.

11. Which word rhymes with **live**? _____

12. Which word starts with a vowel? _____

Name _____

Spelling Spree

Unscramble the letters in each Spelling Word.

Write the word on the line.

1. elin _____

2. ahve _____

3. ltae _____

4. eta _____

5. sdei _____

6. maes _____

7. dame _____

8. idhe _____

9. vige _____

10. zies _____

11. nfie _____

12. iteb _____

Spelling Words

1. bite
2. late
3. size
4. made
5. side
6. ate
7. fine
8. same
9. hide
10. line
11. give*
12. have*

Name _____

Proofreading and Writing

Proofreading Find and circle four Spelling Words that are spelled wrong in this puppet show. Write each word correctly.

1. bite
2. late
3. size
4. made
5. side
6. ate
7. fine
8. same
9. hide
10. line
11. give*
12. have*

Mouse: I made a cake for Beth.

Duck: Great! We can givve it to her when she gets home.

Mouse: Look at the cake! Someone took a bitt out of this side.

Duck: It looks fien to me.

Mouse: Maybe I should cut that piece off and make the cake a smaller siz.

Duck: I have a better idea. Let's eat this cake and make a new one for Beth.

_____   _____

_____

Write an Opinion Write a few sentences telling what you think happened to the cake. Use another sheet of paper. Use Spelling Words from your list.

52   Theme 1: **Silly Stories**

Word Meanings

Read the two meanings for each word. Then write a sentence for each meaning. The first one has been done for you.

Example: land

> The **land** is the ground.
>
> To **land** is to come down.

The farmer's land is flat.

We watch the plane land.

back

> The **back** is the rear part of the body.
> To come **back** is to return.

1. _____

2. _____

tire

> A **tire** is a circle of rubber.
> To **tire** is to get sleepy.

3. _____

4. _____

Name _____

Action Parts Puzzle

Color red the puzzle pieces with action parts.

in the bathroom

books in the library

walked across the room

Mrs. Brown and her animals

cooked a huge meal

drove to the store

took a trip

the barn

to the lake

told a story

Now write complete sentences for the puzzle parts that you colored red.

1. _____

2. _____

3. _____

4. _____

5. _____

54 Theme 1: **Silly Stories**

Name _____

Animal Actions

Complete each sentence to tell what the animals are doing.

Be sure to put a period at the end of each sentence.

> purrs as it naps under a tree
>
> trot across the field to the barn
>
> hops on the lily pads in the pond
>
> barks at the ducks
>
> quack loudly

1. Some horses _____

   _____

2. The ducks in the pond _____

   _____

3. The frog _____

   _____

4. A big brown dog _____

   _____

5. The cat _____

   _____

Listing Actions

Here is a list of things the animals did while Mrs. Brown was gone. Circle *Yes* or *No* to tell whether each item has an action part.

What the Animals Did

1. One of her gowns.	Yes	No
2. The yak and cow.	Yes	No
3. The ducks rang the doorbell many times.	Yes	No
4. The pigs painted the house.	Yes	No
5. A snack from food in the pantry.	Yes	No

Add words to the items that did not have action parts. Write the complete sentences on the lines below.

_____

_____

_____

_____

_____

Name _____

Organizing a Journal Entry

What is the date of the journal entry?

What happened to me that I want to write about?

Who was there? What did they say?

Who	What They Said

What happened?

What describing words tell about the events?

Events	Describing Words

Name _____

Goldilocks's Journal

After Goldilocks visited the three bears, she wrote this plan for a journal entry. On a separate sheet of paper, write your own journal entry. Use this plan to help you.

Date

What do I want to write about?

Who was there?   What did they say?

Who ──────────────→ What They Said

Events → Describing Words

Name _____

Choosing the Best Answer

Use what you have learned about taking tests to help you answer these questions. You may go back to **Dragon Gets By** if you need to. This practice will help you when you take this kind of test.

Read each question. Choose the best answer. Fill in the circle beside your answer.

1 Where is Dragon at the beginning of the story?

   ○ at the store

   ○ at home

   ○ in his car

2 Why does Dragon go to the store?

   ○ He loves to shop for different kinds of food.

   ○ He is a wise shopper.

   ○ He doesn't have any food in his cupboard.

3 What happens when Dragon tries to put the food that he bought in his car?

   ○ The food does not fit.

   ○ He sees that he forgot to buy fudge pops.

   ○ The car rolls down the hill.

Name _____

Choosing the Best Answer

continued

4 Where is Dragon when he eats all the food he bought?

   ○ at home

   ○ in the parking lot

   ○ in the store

5 Why can't Dragon fit in his car?

   ○ He ate too much food.

   ○ He had too many bags of food.

   ○ He grew too tall.

6 At the end of the story, what does Dragon find when he opens his cupboard?

   ○ The cupboard is full of food.

   ○ His car is in the cupboard.

   ○ The cupboard is still empty.

Name _____

Spelling Review

Write Spelling Words from the list to answer the questions.

1–14. Which words have the short **a**, **e**, **i**, **o**, or **u** sound?

1. _____   8. _____

2. _____   9. _____

3. _____   10. _____

4. _____   11. _____

5. _____   12. _____

6. _____   13. _____

7. _____   14. _____

15–20. Which words have the long **a** or long **i** sound?

15. _____   18. _____

16. _____   19. _____

17. _____   20. _____

Spelling Words

1. am
2. hide
3. made
4. his
5. nut
6. dig
7. job
8. size
9. fox
10. sat
11. fun
12. late
13. hug
14. wet
15. mop
16. went
17. leg
18. bite
19. ran
20. ate

Name _____

Spelling Spree

Silly Scramble Change the order of letters in the words below to make Spelling Words.

1. tale _____

2. eat _____

3. gel _____

4. dame _____

1. went
2. bite
3. ran
4. fox
5. made
6. ate
7. nut
8. late
9. leg
10. fun

Rhyme Time Finish the sentences. Write a Spelling Word that rhymes with the word in dark print.

5. Mom and I _____ to buy a new **tent**.

6. I saw a _____ peek out of the **box**.

7. A hungry bird took a _____ from my **kite**.

8. Jason _____ to get a **pan**.

9. Just for _____, let's draw a red **sun**!

10. I found a _____ inside of a **hut**.

Name _____

Proofreading and Writing

Proofreading Circle four Spelling Words below that are wrong. Then write them correctly.

I yam a squirrel named Sam. I like to play with my friend Tree. I give her a big hugg each day. We have lots of fun. I hied in her branches. She always finds me! When it is wett, she keeps me dry.

1. _____   3. _____

2. _____   4. _____

Spelling Words

1. dig
2. wet
3. sat
4. his
5. mop
6. job
7. hide
8. size
9. am
10. hug

Finish the Story Write Spelling Words to complete the sentences in this story.

Sam the squirrel 5. _____ in Tree. He ate 6. _____ last nut. He would have to 7. _____ up more later. Today's 8. _____ was to clean up under Tree. "Tree," Sam asked, "where is the 9. _____ ?"

"You can't use that!" Tree said. "You're too small in 10. _____ .

Finish the Story On another sheet of paper, write a letter from Tree. Use the Spelling Review words.

Name

Nature Walk

What about nature and the outdoors do you enjoy most? Describe an event or activity that you have seen or enjoyed doing outdoors.

_____

_____

_____

_____

_____

_____

_____

Complete the word web with words and phrases that describe a nature walk you have taken.

Name _____

Nature Walk

Fill in the chart as you read the stories.

	Where does the nature walk in the story take place?	What do some of the characters see and learn about on their nature walk?
Henry and Mudge and the Starry Night		
Exploring Parks with Ranger Dockett		
Around the Pond: Who's Been Here?		

Name _____

Go Long

Say the name of each picture. Circle the picture of the
word that has the long vowel sound and the CVCe pattern.

 cub   cube

Complete each pair of sentences using the words
in the boxes.

1. My _____ is part of my face.

   My teacher wrote me a _____.

nose	note

2. It is not polite to be _____ to
   other people.
   Follow every school _____.

rule	rude

3. My brother's name is _____.

   _____are my socks.

These	Pete

4. The flag is on the _____.

   Byron told a funny _____.

pole	joke

5. The store is _____.

   Are you _____ today?

closing	voting

Name _____

Tiger and Giraffe Sounds

There are two sounds for the letter **g**. It can

sound like the **g** in the middle of ,

or it can sound like the **g** at the beginning of

 .

Word Bank

gone	gym	huge	large	village
pig	began	gave	giant	wagon

**Write each word from the box under the word that has
the matching *g* sound.**

Tiger   **Giraffe**

1. _____   6. _____

2. _____   7. _____

3. _____   8. _____

4. _____   9. _____

5. _____   10. _____

68   Theme 2: **Nature Walk**

Name _____

Puzzle Play

Fill in the puzzle with words from the box that fit the clues.

Word Bank

quiet　　even　　straight　　beautiful　　year

Across

1. Last _____ we went camping at Star Lake.
2. It is so _____ there.
3. At night it is very _____.

Down

4. You cannot _____ hear a bird chirping.
5. As soon as it gets dark I go _____ to sleep!

Think of a quiet and beautiful place. Write a sentence about it.

6. _____

_____

_____

Camping Words

Use words from the box to label the pictures.

Vocabulary

backpack

lanterns

hike

campfire

tent

1.
2. _____
3. _____
4. _____
5. _____

Write a sentence about camping. Use some of the words above.

6. _____

_____

_____

Name _____

Graphic Organizer

Venn Diagram As you read the story, write what Henry's mother is like, what Henry's father is like, and how both are the same.

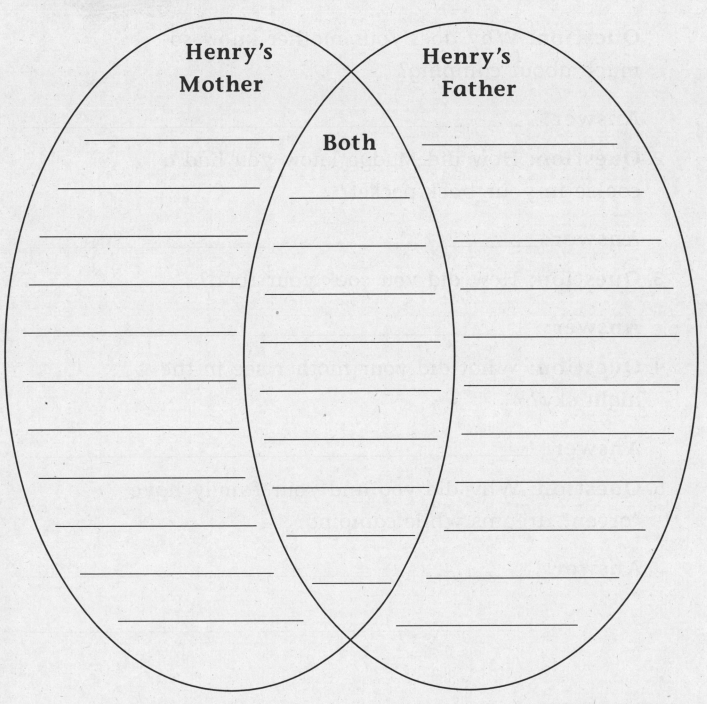

Henry's
Mother

Both

Henry's
Father

Name _____

Interviewing Henry

Write the answers Henry might give to these questions.

1. **Question:** Why does your mother know so much about camping?

   Answer: _____

2. **Question:** How did Mudge know you had a cookie in your back pocket?

   Answer: _____

3. **Question:** How did you cook your food?

   Answer: _____

4. **Question:** What did your mother see in the night sky?

   Answer: _____

5. **Question:** Why did you and your family have "green" dreams while camping?

   Answer: _____

   _____

72   Theme 2: **Nature Walk**

Compare and Contrast

Read the story. Complete the diagram on page 74.

Alike and Different

Lori and her parents like the outdoors. One sunny Saturday, the family decided to go hiking at a nearby park. They dressed in their hiking clothes and got their backpacks. Mom put food in her backpack. She told Lori that they would have a picnic lunch. Dad packed a picnic blanket, the first-aid kit, and the park map in his backpack. Lori put only one thing in her backpack. It was her cat, Sprinkles!

The family walked to the park with Sprinkles peeking out from Lori's backpack. In the park, Mom and Dad waved to other hikers they passed. Dad talked about the plants they saw. He knew a lot about plants. Mom looked over her shoulder to check on Lori and Sprinkles.

After a while, the family stopped to rest. Sprinkles took a nap. Mom pointed to some wild animals she saw. Suddenly, Dad decided to be silly. He pretended to be the animals. He scampered like a squirrel, hopped like a rabbit, and flapped his arms like a bird. Lori and her mom laughed.

Name _____

Compare and Contrast
(continued)

Think about the story you read. Then fill in the chart to tell how Lori's mother and father are alike and different.

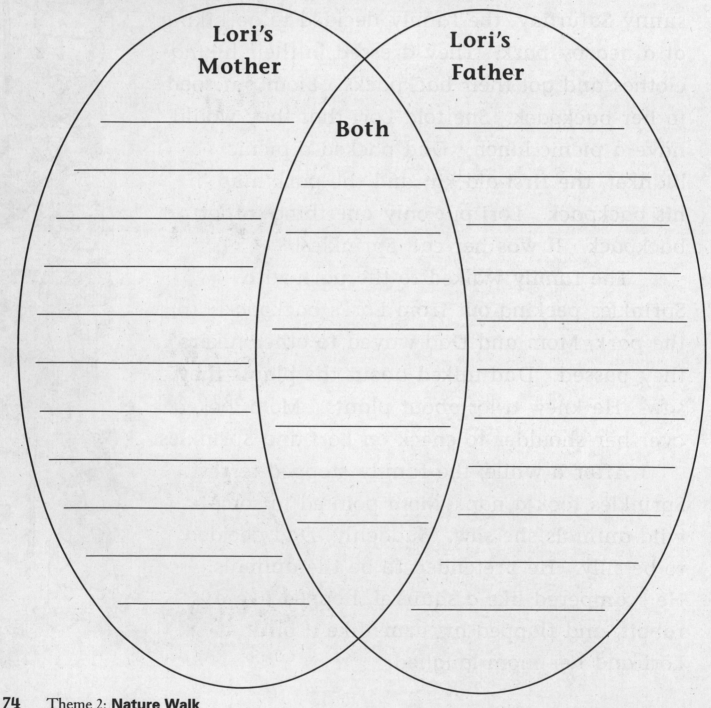

Lori's
Mother

Both

Lori's
Father

Name _____

Fishing for Vowels

Read the sentences. Draw a circle around each word that has a long vowel sound and the CVCe pattern.

1. My friend and I live by the lake.
2. We are both nine years old.
3. We are about the same size.
4. I usually sleep late.
5. He comes to wake me up.
6. Then we go fishing and play hide and seek.
7. Sometimes we race our toy cars.
8. My friend is nice.
9. I like him very much.

Now write each word you circled in the fish that has the same vowel sound and the CVCe pattern.

safe

hide

Name _____

Match the Sound

Most of the Spelling Words have the long
vowel sound spelled with the VCe pattern.

► The words **one** and **goes** do not follow
this rule.

**Write each Spelling Word under the word with
the same vowel sound and VCe pattern.**

1. bone
2. robe
3. use
4. these
5. rope
6. note
7. cute
8. close
9. hope
10. those
11. one*
12. goes*

Home

_____

_____

_____

_____

_____

_____

Cube

_____

Pete

**Write the words that are not spelled with the VCe pattern or do not
have the long vowel sound.**

_____   _____

Name _____

Spelling Spree

Write a Spelling Word for each clue.

1. It rhymes with **flute**.
   It begins like **cup**. _____

2. It rhymes with **nose**.
   It begins like **get**. _____

3. It rhymes with **hose**.
   It begins like **clock**. _____

4. It rhymes with **cone**.
   It begins like **bat**. _____

5. It rhymes with **keys**.
   It begins like **them**. _____

6. It rhymes with **soap**.
   It begins like **home**. _____

7. It rhymes with **boat**.
   It begins like **name**. _____

8. It rhymes with **rose**.
   It begins like **that**. _____

1. bone
2. robe
3. use
4. these
5. rope
6. note
7. cute
8. close
9. hope
10. those
11. one*
12. goes*

Name _____

Proofreading and Writing

Here is a letter Henry might have written. Circle four Spelling Words that are not spelled correctly. Write them correctly on the lines.

1. bone
2. robe
3. use
4. these
5. rope
6. note
7. cute
8. close
9. hope
10. those
11. one*
12. goes*

Dear Mom and Dad,

Thank you for taking Mudge and me camping. The next time we go camping, I'm going to use a stronger rupe on my backpack. The one I did uoos didn't work very well.

I'm also going to hide wun bone in my roob pocket. I want to see if Mudge can find it like he found the cookie. I hope you like reading this note. Mudge helped me write it.

Love,

Henry and Mudge

Henry

_____ _____

_____ _____

 Write a Note **On another sheet of paper, write a note to someone. Use Spelling Words from the list.**

Name _____

One + One = One

A **compound word** is made up of two shorter words. The word **campfire** is a compound word.

camp + fire = campfire

Draw a line from the word on the left to the word on the right to make a compound word.

1. sun   storm
2. thunder   rise
3. water   bow
4. rain   fall

Now use each compound word in a sentence.

5. _____

6. _____

7. _____

8. _____

Sentence or Question?

► A telling sentence tells about someone or something. It begins with a capital letter and ends with a period.

► A question asks about someone or something. It begins with a capital letter and ends with a question mark.

Unscramble the words to make a telling sentence or a question.

Remember to use capital letters and the correct end marks.

1. fun is camping _____

   _____

2. sleep a we in tent _____

   _____

3. like you go camping to do _____

   _____

Write a telling sentence about the picture.

4. _____

   _____

Write a question about the picture.

5. _____

   _____

Name _____

Sentence to Question

**Read each telling sentence. Turn it into a question.
Use words from the box. The first one has been
done for you.**

Word Bank

Where

Who

When

What

1. Some people love to go camping.

   What do some people love to do? _____

2. It is fun to go camping in the summer.

   _____

3. My dad likes to sleep in a tent.

   _____

4. I like to go camping at Star Lake.

   _____

What can you do on a camping trip? Write two telling sentences.

5. _____

   _____

   _____

Name _____

Change It!

**Change these telling sentences to questions.
Remember to begin with a capital letter
and include the correct end mark.**

1. Henry and Mudge went camping in August.

   _____

2. Mudge is Henry's big dog.

   _____

3. Henry's parents took Henry and Mudge camping.

   _____

   _____

**Change these questions into telling sentences. Remember to
begin with a capital letter and include the correct end mark.**

4. Did Mudge have a backpack?

   _____

5. Did Henry want to see a bear?

   _____

   _____

6. Did Henry and his family go hiking?

   _____

Name _____

Questions and Answers

**Write an answer to each question. Remember to
write complete sentences.**

1. **Question:** Where did Henry and his family go camping?

   Answer: _____

   _____

2. **Question:** What did Mudge carry in his backpack?

   Answer: _____

   _____

3. **Question:** What did Henry's father bring with him?

   Answer: _____

   _____

Name _____

What Do You See?

Look at the picture. Read the questions and answers.
Rewrite the answers to make them complete sentences.

1. **Question:** Which animals are sleeping in the cave?
   Answer: the bears

   _____

   _____

2. **Question:** What are the raccoons doing?
   Answer: catching fish

   _____

   _____

3. **Question:** What is the bird doing?
   Answer: sitting in a tree

   _____

   _____

4. **Question:** Which animal is standing under a tree?
   Answer: the deer

   _____

   _____

Name _____

Revising Your Description

Put a check next to the sentences that tell about your writing.

Superstar

☐ I told the reader what I am describing.

☐ My description tells how something looks, feels, sounds, tastes, and smells.

☐ My description uses details to make a clear picture for the reader.

☐ I wrote in complete sentences.

Rising Star

☐ I need to tell what I am describing.

☐ I need to add words that tell how something looks, feels, sounds, tastes, and smells.

☐ I could add some details to make a clearer picture for the reader.

☐ Some of my sentences are not complete.

Writing Sentences

Read each group of words. Write the group of words that is a sentence.

1. All kinds of people come to the river.
   All kinds of people.

   _____

2. In the river.
   My dad likes to catch fish in the river.

   _____

3. Different birds and bugs.
   I see different birds and bugs here.

   _____

4. Life on the river changes from season to season.
   From season to season.

   _____

Think of an outdoor spot you enjoy. Write two sentences about it. Make sure your sentence tells what someone or something is doing.

5. _____

6. _____

Name _____

Spelling Words

These Spelling Words are words that you use in your writing. Look carefully at how they are spelled. Write the missing letters in the Spelling Words below. Use the words in the box.

1. o____

7. fr____m

2. w_____t

8. d_____s

3. a____

9. h_____

4. h_____

10. th____r____

5. c_____e

11. g_____s

6. ____f

12. the_____

Spelling Words

1. on
2. am
3. come
4. if
5. does
6. goes
7. from
8. his
9. want
10. her
11. their
12. there

Write the Spelling Words below.

_____   _____

_____   _____

_____   _____

_____   _____

_____   _____

their

there

Name _____

Spelling Spree

Write a Spelling Word to finish each riddle.

Spelling Words

1. on
2. am
3. come
4. if
5. does
6. goes
7. from
8. his
9. want
10. her
11. their
12. there

1. I'm made _____ wood.
You can write with me.

2. I swim _____ in the lake.
I have scales and fins.

3. I _____ out at night.
I rhyme with soon.

4. I _____ on a wall.
You can see yourself in me.

5. I am _____ best friend.
She likes me.
I bark and run.

Write the Spelling Word that matches the clue.

6. the opposite of **off** _____

7. to do something _____

8. to go somewhere _____

9. to wish for something _____

10. shows something belongs _____
to some people

Name _____

Proofreading and Writing

Proofreading Find and circle misspelled Spelling Words below. Then write each word correctly.

The little bird landed on the fence post. He had cume from the woods. His feathers were brown with speckles of black. "Ef he is hungry, he will wunt the seeds," I thought.

Suddenly he swooped down onto the deck. He pecked the tiny, hard seeds I had thrown thair. Suddenly, he lifted hiz head as if he heard a sound. He flapped his wings and flew off into the woods.

Spelling Words

1. on
2. am
3. come
4. if
5. does
6. goes
7. from
8. his
9. want
10. her
11. their
12. there

_____ _____

_____ _____

_____

Write and Draw an Animal On another sheet of paper, draw pictures of some animals you might see in your backyard. Write a sentence below each picture that tells about the animal. Use as many Spelling Words as you can.

Name _____

Name That!

Write the name of each picture. Then circle the consonant cluster.

Example:

__(pr)esent__

1. _____

2. _____

3. _____

4. _____

5. _____

6. _____

7. _____

8. _____

Name _____

Camping Trip

Read the story. Circle the words in which the letter *c* makes the same sound you hear at the beginning of the word *sand*.

Juan and Hal went to the park to camp. They were far from the city. They carried their equipment to the pond and set up their tent near a fence. It was a cold night, so they collected wood and made a big fire. Their faces glowed in the firelight. They cooked hot dogs. Then they ate cookies and went to sleep. In the morning there was a thin layer of ice on the pond. But Juan and Hal were warm in their tent!

Now read the story again. Draw a line under the words in which *c* makes the same sound you hear at the beginning of *cup*.

Name _____

A Ranger's Day

Read what one park ranger did at work today.

Then answer the questions.

10:00 Collect seeds to plant later this week.

12:30 Eat lunch with the other rangers.

2:00 Check on the baby deer at the
petting zoo.

3:00 *Important: Take class to plant trees.

5:00 Go home after this busy day!

1. How did the park ranger stay in touch with the other rangers?

_____

_____

2. What young animals did he check on?

_____

_____

3. When will the seeds be planted?

_____

_____

4. What kind of day did the park ranger have?

_____

Name _____

A Special Job

Use words from the box to finish the sentences. They will tell about a very special job.

> ### Vocabulary
>
> exploring habitat protect ranger tours urban

1. A park _____ has many jobs.

2. Some rangers work in _____ parks.

3. They lead people on _____ to see plants and animals.

4. Rangers must know many things about the _____ around them.

5. They must enjoy _____ the natural world.

6. It is their job to _____ the plants and animals.

Name ______________________________

K-W-L Chart

Complete this chart.

What I Know

Rangers take care of parks.

____

____

____

What I Want to Know

____

____

____

____

What I Learned

____

____

____

____

Name _____

Describe the Job

Read the want ad. Write a word to complete each sentence.

Park Ranger Needed!

Central Park needs a new ranger. To do this job well, you must be able to lead people on _____ of the park. You must keep in _____ with other rangers. You must _____ trees, help people follow the park _____, and teach classes about the plants and _____ found in the park.

What kind of person would make a good park ranger? Finish this sentence.

A good park ranger is someone who

_____

_____

_____

_____

Name _____

Fact and Opinion

Read the story. Answer the questions on page 97.

The Park in Winter

The park is a fun place to go in the winter. When the pond freezes, it is a good place to ice skate. There is a small building by the pond. Inside the building it is nice and warm. You can even buy delicious hot chocolate there.

When it snows, bring your sled. The hill is a good place for sledding. The snow on the hill is soft and deep. Be careful around the trees. You don't want to crash! Sometimes there are twenty children sledding on the hill. They wear hats, gloves, and boots to stay warm. Their sleds are red, green, blue, and yellow. There are so many colors! Sledding is fun for everyone.

Right after the snow falls, the park is very quiet. The snow helps to make it quiet. But if you listen, you might hear a woodpecker pecking an old tree. It is looking for bugs to eat. A busy woodpecker is noisy.

Name _____

Fact and Opinion (continued)

Think about what you read. Then write facts or opinions from the story.

Write one fact about the building.

_____

Write an opinion about hot chocolate.

_____

Write one fact about the children sledding.

_____

Write an opinion about sledding.

_____

Write one fact about woodpeckers.

_____

Write one opinion about woodpeckers.

_____

What do you like about the park in winter?
Write one fact and one opinion.

Fact: _____

Opinion: _____

Name _____

Vowel Fun

Draw a circle around each word that has a long vowel sound and the CVCe pattern.

some   home

holes   pole   these

hear   huge   store

sure   cute

Use the words you circled to finish these sentences.

1. The park is _____ to many animals.

2. Once I saw a _____ little frog.

3. Some birds live in _____ in the trees.

4. I passed a turtle sitting on a log that looked

   like a long _____.

5. A horse was standing next to a

   _____ tree.

6. All _____ animals make the park

   a fun place.

Name _____

Consonant Clusters

A **consonant cluster** is two consonant letters whose sounds are blended together. Some consonant clusters are **tr**, **sw**, **st**, **cl**, **xt**, **br**, and **gl**.

Write the Spelling Words that begin with a consonant cluster.

frog

_____ _____

_____ _____

_____ _____

Write the Spelling Words that end with a consonant cluster.

bird

_____ _____

_____

Name _____

Spelling Spree

Combine letters from the two frogs to make the Spelling Words that begin with two consonants.

1. trip
2. swim
3. step
4. nest
5. club
6. stone
7. next
8. brave
9. glad
10. lost

tr sw st
cl br gl

ip im ep ad
ub one ave

1. _____   5. _____

2. _____   6. _____

3. _____   7. _____

4. _____

Combine letters from the two birds to make Spelling Words that end with two consonants.

ne lo

st xt

8. _____   10. _____

9. _____

100   Theme 2: **Nature Walk**

Name _____

Proofreading and Writing

Proofreading **Read the sentences below. Find three Spelling Words that are not spelled correctly. Draw a circle around the words. Then write each word correctly.**

What to do on the class field trip:

1. Look for a nets.

2. Look under a ston for bugs.

3. Find the place where the fish smim.

1. trip
2. swim
3. step
4. nest
5. club
6. stone
7. next
8. brave
9. glad
10. lost

1. _____

2. _____

3. _____

Writing **What kinds of things does a bird do? Write two sentences about a bird. Use some of your Spelling Words in your sentences.**

_____

_____

_____

Name _____

Match the Opposites

Draw a line from each word on the left to a word on the right that has the opposite meaning.

1. sad

2. lost

3. never

4. thick

5. below

6. start

found

finish

happy

thin

always

above

Think of words that mean the opposite of each of the words below. Write those words on the lines.

7. front _____

8. soft _____

9. dark _____

10. asleep _____

Name _____

Find the Commands

A command
► is a sentence that tells someone what to do
► has an understood subject **you**
► begins with a capital letter and ends with a period

Read the sentences below. If a sentence is a command, write C on the line next to it.

_____ 1. Who likes to go to the park?

_____ 2. Dogs run in the park.

_____ 3. Keep your dog on a leash.

_____ 4. Don't throw balls near the pond.

_____ 5. The park is always open.

_____ 6. Don't pick the flowers.

_____ 7. Some people like to run in the park.

_____ 8. Keep your bike on the trail.

_____ 9. When can we meet the park ranger?

_____ 10. Use the trash cans.

Name _____

Command Some Fun

Read each sentence about the park. Then change it into a command.

1. I want you to have fun in the park.

_____

2. You can meet the other park rangers at noon.

_____

3. I think you should listen to the birds.

_____

4. Everyone can take a picture of the deer.

_____

5. You should stay on the trail.

_____

Name _____

Use Good Manners

Read this note that a park ranger wrote.
Look for places to make it more polite.

We are going on a field trip to the pond. Be ready for a big adventure. This trip will be fun. Wear rubber boots or old shoes. Your feet might get wet. Bring a sweater or jacket. The air is cool in the fall. Don't bring any more than you need. But bring a smile!

Write the note again. Add the word *please* in five places.
Use capital letters and end marks correctly.

_____

_____

_____

_____

_____

_____

_____

Name _____

Choose a Topic

How do you choose a topic to write about?
You can choose a topic you already know about
or want to know about.

Write three topics you already know about.

1. _____

2. _____

3. _____

Choose one of these topics and write it inside the box in the middle. Then write something you know about this topic in each of the other four boxes.

Write a sentence that tells what your paragraph will be about.

_____

Name _____

Adding Details

This park ranger needs your help. Add details to his invitation to make it more interesting. The birds show where to add details. Write the new invitation below.

There are many things to see in the park!
In the ⬚ pond, there are ⬚ ducks swimming. Many ⬚ mushrooms grow under the ⬚ trees. Squirrels are getting ready for a ⬚ winter. Let me show you around the park.

Come to the park!

_____

_____

_____

_____

_____

Word Maker

Read the words on the left that end with double consonants or the letters _ck_. Add letters to make new words. Use the clues to help you. The first one has been done for you.

pill + ow =

1. pill   what you rest your head on   pillow

2. rock   a kind of chair   _____

3. dress   you put this on salad   _____

4. buck   use it to carry water   _____

5. crack   something to eat   _____

6. yell   the color of a lemon   _____

7. skill   a pan for cooking   _____

8. less   something to be learned   _____

9. rock   a ship that shoots up into the air _____

10. fell   another word for man   _____

Name _____

What a Great Day!

Read the story below. Use the words in the box to finish the story. You will use each word two times.

Word Bank			
across	brother	great	stand

My _____ and I went to the

pond. We walked _____ the

bridge. I asked him to _____

next to a tall pine tree. I took his picture. My

_____ looked small next to that

_____ big tree. He could not

_____ still for very long. When

we looked _____ the pond, we

saw our father. He was bringing us lunch. He

gave us some _____ sandwiches.

We had fun together at the pond.

Theme 2: **Nature Walk**   109

Name _____

What's the Word?

Take a trip to the pond. Use words from the box to answer each question.

Word Bank

bank   crater   edge   moss   path   shallow

1. What do you follow to get to the pond?

_____

2. What do you call the line where the water

begins or ends? _____

3. What might you see growing under a tree?

_____

4. What must you climb down to get to the

pond? _____

5. What is another name for a hole in the

ground? _____

6. What word describes water that is not

very deep? _____

Name _____

Around the Pond Chart

As you read the story, complete the chart below by writing other categories of animals that Cammy and William found at the pond.

Birds	
_____ _____ _____	_____ _____ _____
_____ _____ _____	_____ _____ _____

Name _____

Follow the Clues!

Finish the chart. Write either the clues or the names of the animals that Cammy and William found at the pond.

Clue	Animal
1. white feathers stuck to bark	_____
2. _____	raccoon
3. _____	beaver
4. crater on sandy bottom of water	_____
5. _____	garter snake
6. _____	great blue heron
7. pile of mussel shells in mud	_____

Name _____

Categorize and Classify

Read the story below. Complete the chart on page 114.

Around the Swamp

Wanda likes to visit the swamp. A swamp is a place that is very wet. Wanda's dad takes her around the swamp in his boat. They float under willow trees and gum trees.

Many animals live in the swamp. Wanda looks out for cottonmouth snakes. She knows they are very dangerous. Wanda's dad likes to watch for birds. He points out the hawks and vultures in the sky. There are many animals in the swamp that they never see. The fox only comes out at night, and the bobcat stays away from people. There is bass in the water, but the water is too dark to see the fish.

From the boat, Wanda can see turtles. The turtles lie in the sun and hardly move. Once they saw a raccoon catching a fish. But the most exciting day at the swamp was when they saw two black bear cubs running between the trees.

Name _____

Categorize and Classify
(continued)

After you've read the story, complete the chart below.

At the bottom of the chart, make up your own category

about the swamp. Write some examples.

Category	Examples
Trees	
Snake	
Birds	
An Animal That Comes out at Night	
Fish	
An Animal That Eats Fish	

Name _____

Blend the Sounds

Word Bank

| trip | stop | play | fly | dry | snow |

Write each word in the box under the picture whose
name begins with the same sound. Then write two other
words that begin with the same sound.

1. _____

2. _____

3. _____

4. _____

5. _____

6. _____

7. _____

8. _____

9. _____

10. _____

11. _____

12. _____

13. _____

14. _____

15. _____

16. _____

17. _____

18. _____

Name _____

Double Consonants

In words like **bell**, **off**, and **dress**, the final consonant sound is spelled with two letters that are the same.

Write the Spelling Words that end with the same double consonant as *ball*.

1. _____

2. _____

3. _____

4. _____

5. _____

Write the Spelling Words that end with the same double consonant as *dress*.

6. _____

7. _____

Write the three Spelling Words that remain.

8. _____

9. _____

10. _____

Spelling Words

1. bell
2. off
3. all
4. mess
5. add
6. hill
7. well
8. egg
9. will
10. grass

116   Theme 2: **Nature Walk**

Name _____

Spelling Spree

Write the Spelling Word that answers each riddle.

You can hear me ring.
What am I?

1. bell

_____

2. off

You must clean me up.
What am I?

3. all

4. mess

_____

5. add

If you drop me, my shell will break.
What am I?

6. hill

7. well

_____

8. egg

Climb up me. Roll back down.
What am I?

9. will

10. grass

_____

Water me to keep me green.
What am I?

_____

Use a bucket to get my water.
What am I?

_____

Name _____

Proofreading and Writing

Proofreading Circle four Spelling Words that are spelled wrong. Then write each word correctly.

Spelling Words

Dear Grandma,

   Today I walked to the pond with three friends. We alll sang as we walked. We passed some workers. They were deciding on where to ad more paths to the pond. We had fun watching a group of baby birds fly uff. We also saw a tiny blue egg in a nest. Soon a bird wil hatch from it!

                         Love,
                         Maria

Spelling Words

1. bell
2. off
3. all
4. mess
5. add
6. hill
7. well
8. egg
9. will
10. grass

1. _____

2. _____

3. _____

4. _____

Write a Letter On a separate piece of paper, write a letter to someone in your family. Tell them what you would like to see or do at the pond. Use Spelling Words from the list.

Name _____

What Do You Mean?

Read the two meanings for each word. Then write a sentence for each meaning.

Example: **can**

A **can** is something that soup comes in.

The word **can** means to be able to do something.

I will open the can.

Mary can read hard books.

watch: A **watch** is a small clock worn on the wrist.
To **watch** means to look at something.

1. _____

2. _____

tie: A **tie** is something men wear.
To **tie** means to fasten or close up something.

3. _____

4. _____

bark: **Bark** is what dogs do.
Bark is the covering on a tree.

5. _____

6. _____

Name _____

Excitement at the Pond

► A command is a sentence that tells someone to do something.

► An exclamation is a sentence that shows a strong feeling, such as surprise or fear.

Read each sentence. Write C if it is a command.
Write E if it is an exclamation.

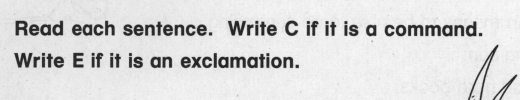

_____ 1. Ming: I see a muskrat!

_____ 2. John: Let's take a picture of it!

_____ 3. Ming: Be very quiet.

_____ 4. John: Take a picture now.

Write each group of words as a command or an exclamation. Use a capital letter and the correct end mark.

5. don't get close to the pond

_____

6. be careful where you step

_____

7. the water is cold

_____

Name _____

Who's at the Pond?

**Under each picture write what Jenny is saying. Each
sentence should be an *exclamation*.**

1. _____   2. _____

_____   _____

**Pedro is at the pond with his mother. Look at the pictures.
Under each picture write what Pedro's mother says to him.
Each sentence should be a *command*.**

3. _____   4. _____

_____   _____

Theme 2: **Nature Walk**   121

Name _____

It's a Field Trip!

**Read the announcement for the field trip to the pond.
Each sentence should be an exclamation or a command.
Check the capital letters and end marks for each
sentence. Circle any mistakes.**

We're going on a field trip. plan to be gone
all morning? bring a sweater! bring a snack?
We're ready to have a good time.

**In the space below, write the announcement using
capital letters and end marks correctly.**

Name _____

Learning Log

As you read the story, write a learning log entry for one of the pages in the story.

Notes About the Story	My Thoughts About My Notes
_____	_____
_____	_____
_____	_____
_____	_____
_____	_____
_____	_____
_____	_____
_____	_____
_____	_____
_____	_____

Name _____

Tell More About the Story

Read the sentences in column A that tell about the story.

In column B, add more details to each sentence. Write your new

sentence on the line.

Story: Around the Pond	
A **Telling About the Story**	**B** **Adding More Details**
William and Cammy see white feathers.	_____ _____ _____ _____
A tree has fallen.	_____ _____ _____ _____
Cammy saw a shape on the tree.	_____ _____ _____

Name _____

Filling in the Blank

Use what you have learned about taking tests to help you complete fill-in-the-blank sentences with the correct answer. This practice will help you when you take this kind of test.

Read the sentence. Fill in the circle next to the answer that best completes the sentence.

1 Henry's mother knew more about _____ than his father.

○ singing   ○ camping

○ bears   ○ waterfalls

2 Both Henry and Mudge _____.

○ saw a fish jump out of a stream

○ smelled a deer

○ ate an oatmeal cookie

○ loved to go camping

3 Everyone in Henry's family had a _____, even Mudge.

○ cookie   ○ lantern

○ backpack   ○ tent

Name _____

Filling in the Blank continued

4 Henry did not like it when his father _____.

○ sang love songs

○ cooked camp food

○ set up the tent

○ built the campfire

5 At night, Henry and his parents looked at the _____ in the sky.

○ rainbow

○ clouds

○ birds

○ stars

6 Inside the tent, Henry and Mudge _____ just like Henry's parents.

○ got ready to hike

○ snuggled

○ giggled

○ sang love songs

126 Theme 2: **Nature Walk**

Name _____

Spelling Review

Write Spelling Words from the list to answer the questions.

1–7. Which words have the long **a, e, o,** or **u** sound spelled vowel-consonant-e?

1._____   5._____

2._____   6._____

3._____   7._____

4._____

8–15. Which words have the consonant cluster **tr, sw, st, cl, br, gl,** or **xt**?

8._____   12._____

9._____   13._____

10._____   14._____

11._____   15._____

16–22. Which words have double consonants?

16._____   20._____

17._____   21._____

18._____   22._____

19._____

Spelling Words

1. lost
2. these
3. glad
4. grass
5. hope
6. cute
7. trip
8. swim
9. off
10. bone
11. egg
12. next
13. stone
14. mess
15. brave
16. use
17. add
18. club
19. all
20. hill

Name _____

Spelling Spree

Double Delights Write the Spelling Word that answers each question.

Spelling Words

1. bone
2. hill
3. egg
4. swim
5. grass
6. all
7. stone
8. glad
9. club
10. add

1. What can you hike up? _____

2. What grows in yards? _____

3. What does a chicken lay? _____

4. What is the opposite of **none**?

   _____

Riddles Write a Spelling Word to answer each riddle.

5. This is something a dog likes. What is

   this? _____

6. You do this in the water. What is this? _____

7. This is a group you join. What is this? _____

8. You can use this to build. What is this? _____

9. You can do this with numbers. What is this?

   _____

10. If you are happy, you feel this way. What is this?

    _____

Name _____

Proofreading and Writing

Proofreading Circle four Spelling Words that are wrong below. Then write each word correctly.

Dear Gran,

    Yesterday I went on a tripp to the lake with Mom. We saw cyute fish!

    I have to go clean my room now. It is a mes! I hoap you will write back soon.

        Love,

        Celia

Spelling Words

1. brave
2. lost
3. cute
4. use
5. next
6. mess
7. off
8. these
9. hope
10. trip

1. _____ 3. _____

2. _____ 4. _____

Word for Word Write the Spelling Word that means the opposite of each word or words.

5. scared _____   7. waste _____   9. on _____

6. found _____   8. before _____   10. those _____

✏ **Write a Story** Write a story about a family on a nature walk. Write on another sheet of paper. Use the Spelling Review Words.

Name _____

Comparing Fables

Use the chart below to compare the five fables.

	Characters	Main Event	Moral, or Lesson
The Hare and the Tortoise			
The Crow and the Pitcher			
The Grasshopper and the Ants			
Belling the Cat			
The Fly on the Wagon			

Tell which fable was your favorite and why you liked it.

My favorite fable is _____.

I like it because _____

_____.

Name _____

A Fable Character

An animal in one of the fables learns this lesson: *You do not make friends by being greedy.* Write some sentences that tell about the animal who learns that lesson.

_____

_____

_____

_____

Now draw a picture of the animal.

Name _____

My Community

Describe your neighborhood or community. What does it look like? What do people like to do there? What do you like best about your neighborhood or community?

_____

_____

_____

_____

_____

_____

Describe a place in your neighborhood or community that is important to you.

_____

_____

_____

Name _____

Around Town: Neighborhood and Community

Fill in the chart as you read the stories.

	What neighborhood or community places appear in this theme?	Who are some of the community helpers in this theme?
Chinatown		
A Trip to the Firehouse		
Big Bushy Mustache		
Jamaica Louise James		

Name _____

Which Word?

Circle the word that names or describes each picture.
Then use the circled word in a sentence.

1. watch   wash

   _____

2. lunch   bathtub

   _____

3. chain   path

   _____

4. whispering   toothbrush

   _____

5. feather   shopper

   _____

Big, Bigger, or Biggest?

The word under the picture is a base word. On the line under the middle box, add **-er** to the base word. On the line under the last box, add **-est** to the base word. Then draw pictures in the boxes to show the differences in size.

Example:

large _____

larger _____

largest _____

1.

big _____   _____   _____

2.

long _____   _____   _____

Name _____

Matching and Sorting Words

Draw a line from each word to its meaning.

1. during   the season after fall

2. heard   throughout a certain time

3. lion   a large wild cat

4. winter   something done with ears

Word Bank

| during | heard | lion | winter |

Think how the words in each group are alike. Then choose one word from the box to add to each group of words below.

5. seen, smelled, _____

6. before, after, _____

7. summer, spring, _____

8. tiger, panther, _____

Use two of the words from the box in sentences.

9. _____

10. _____

Name _____

Words to Draw

Draw a picture of someone making a delivery at an apartment. Then use each vocabulary word, *delivery* and *apartment*, in a sentence.

1. _____

2. _____

Draw a picture of people using handcarts at a market. Then use each vocabulary word, *handcarts* and *market*, in a sentence.

3. _____

4. _____

Draw a picture of a celebration. Then use the vocabulary word *celebration* in a sentence.

5. _____

Name _____

What I Like Chart

As you read the story, choose pages that show
things you like to see in Chinatown. Write the page
number and a sentence next to it.

What I Like to See in Chinatown

page ___	
page ___	
page ___	
page ___	
page ___	
page ___	
page ___	
page ___	

Name _____

Retelling the Story

Finish each sentence about Chinatown.

1. The person telling this story is _____

_____

2. Tai chi is _____

_____

3. The grandmother makes medicinal soup when

it gets cold outside because _____

_____

4. The boy can barely move in the outdoor

market because _____

_____

5. The boy in the story will march in the parade

next year because _____

_____

Name _____

Making Judgments

Read the story below.

Cowhands

Hank and Charlie are cowhands on a small cattle ranch. Their job is to herd the cows to town to be sold. This means that they must keep the cattle moving in the right direction. They do this by riding their horses beside the herd.

It is a long, dusty ride on the trails to town. Sometimes the dust is very thick. Hank and Charlie wear scarves called bandannas over their noses and mouths to keep the dust out. No matter how dusty it gets, Hank and Charlie must keep track of every cow.

When the sun goes down, Hank and Charlie find a place to camp. The cattle rest for the night. Hank and Charlie cook their dinner over a campfire. A delicious smell fills the air. The two cowhands are tired after a day of hard work. They spread out their sleeping bags and lie down under the stars. The camp is quiet. After a while Hank and Charlie hear a coyote howling in the distance. They both fall asleep as the coyote sings its song.

Name _____

Making Judgments continued

After you have read the story "Cowhands,"
complete the chart below.

I Would / Would Not Like Chart

Things the Characters Do	I Would/Would Not Like This	Reasons Why I Feel This Way
1. _____ _____		
2. _____ _____		
3. _____ _____		
4. _____ _____		
5. _____ _____		

Name _____

Double the Fun

Use the double consonants in the box to finish each word.

Then write the word on the line.

ck	ff	ll	ss

duck

cuff

ball

dress

1. sme____ _____

2. po____et _____

3. gra____ _____

4. waterfa____ _____

5. sna____ _____

6. ski____ _____

7. gla____ _____

8. sni____ing _____

9. clo____ _____

10. cli____ _____

Name _____

Two Letters—One Sound

Each Spelling Word is spelled with **th**, **wh**, **sh**, or **ch**. Each pair of letters stand for one sound.

▶ the **th** sound ⟶ **th**at, mo**th**er, smoo**th**
▶ the **wh** sound ⟶ **wh**y, some**wh**at
▶ the **sh** sound ⟶ **sh**e, friend**sh**ip, wi**sh**
▶ the **ch** sound ⟶ **ch**ild, sear**ch**ing, ri**ch**

Write each Spelling Word under the word with the same sound. The sound may be at the beginning, middle, or end of the word.

whale

chair

_____

_____

thumb

_____

_____

_____

ship

_____

_____

_____

_____

_____

Name _____

Spelling Spree

Word Fun Think how the words in each group are alike. Write the missing Spelling Words.

1. goats, horses, _____

2. rinse, scrub, _____

3. glass, fork, _____

4. lips, tongue, _____

5. throw, bounce, _____

6. learn, school, _____

Write the two Spelling Words that rhyme with each other.

7. _____

8. _____

Name _____

Proofreading and Writing

Proofreading Read the sentences below. Find and circle four Spelling Words that have spelling mistakes. Write them correctly.

1. Buth Grandma and I love to go to Chinatown.

2. We have a hard time deciding wich seafood restaurant we like best.

3. It is fun to watch the fish in the fish tank chace each other.

4. There is no fish fresher thun the fish in Chinatown.

Spelling Words

1. when
2. sheep
3. both
4. then
5. chase
6. teeth
7. teach
8. dish
9. which
10. than
11. wash
12. catch*

_____   _____

_____   _____

Writing Sentences On a separate sheet of paper, write four sentences that tell about a place you like to visit. Use Spelling Words from the list.

Name _____

Knowing Your ABC's

**Read the words in each box. Write the five words in
ABC order.**

Word Bank

| most | morning | move | mother | month |

1. _____   4. _____

2. _____   5. _____

3. _____

Word Bank

| restaurant | read | remember | report | rent |

6. _____   9. _____

7. _____   10. _____

8. _____

Theme 3: **Neighborhood and Community**   147

Name _____

Who? What? Where?

All of the words in the box are naming words, or nouns. Nouns name people, places, and things.

Complete the chart below. Write words from the box to show which nouns name people, places, and things.

Word Bank

slide	city	boy	park	man
playground	swings	woman	monkey bars	girl

People	**Places**	**Things**
1. _____	5. _____	8. _____
2. _____	6. _____	9. _____
3. _____	7. _____	10. _____
4. _____		

Name _____

Chinatown

Grammar Skill Naming
Words (Common Nouns)

Spotlight on Naming Words

Naming words are called nouns. Nouns name
people, places, and things.

**Read each sentence. Underline the nouns that name
people. Circle the nouns that name things. Draw a box
around the nouns that name places.**

1. The baby is in the swing.

2. The pencil and paper
belong to the student.

3. The family is at the beach.

4. The books are on the
shelves in the library.

Name _____

Revising a News Story

Read the newspaper story. When possible, combine two sentences into one to make the story sound better.

Chinese New Year

Chinatown — Today was the Chinese New Year. People who live in Chinatown celebrated. Visitors celebrated. Adults crowded the streets. Children crowded the streets. Boys from the kung fu school marched down the streets. Girls from the kung fu school marched down the streets. The dragon parade was exciting to watch. The lion dance was exciting to watch. The dragon costumes were beautiful. The lion costume was beautiful. Everyone had a good time.

_____

_____

_____

_____

_____

Name _____

Organizing a Story Scene

Write your ideas for a story scene.

Setting — Where does the scene take place?

_____

_____

Characters — Which characters are in the scene?

_____

_____

Actions or Events — What happens in the scene?

_____

_____

Name _____

To Be Exact

Write each sentence. Replace the underlined word with a more exact noun.

Example:

I visited my aunt at her **place**.
I visited my aunt at her **house**.

1. My aunt and I went to an outdoor <u>place</u> to buy

   food. _____

2. There were many different kinds of fresh <u>foods</u>

   there, such as apples and oranges. _____

   _____

3. My aunt bought three pounds of <u>fruit</u> to make a

   pie. _____

4. She paid the <u>person</u> for the fruit we bought.

   _____

5. When we got to my aunt's house, she made the pie

   and baked it in the <u>thing</u>. _____

   _____

Name _____

Revising Your Friendly Letter

Superstar

☐ I included the five parts of a friendly letter.

☐ date   ☐ body   ☐ my name

☐ greeting   ☐ closing

☐ My topic is interesting to the reader.

☐ I used details in an interesting way.

☐ My letter shows something about me.

☐ I used different kinds of sentences.

Rising Star

☐ I included these parts of a friendly letter.

☐ date   ☐ body   ☐ my name

☐ greeting   ☐ closing

☐ I could add some details to tell more.

☐ My sentences are too much the same.

Name _____

Different Kinds of Sentences

Read each sentence. Then write each sentence with the correct end mark.

1. I am very happy

   _____

2. Did you find my puppy

   _____

3. We went for a walk

   _____

4. This is a big surprise

   _____

Write a telling sentence about a dog.

_____

_____

Name _____

Spelling Words

These Spelling Words are words that you use in your writing. Look carefully at how they are spelled. Write the missing letters in the Spelling Words below. Use the words in the box.

1. n____m____

2. o____

3. t_____e

4. w_____t

5. m____s_____f

6. w____nt

7. wh____t

8. t_____

9. d____

10. l____tt_____

11. t____

12. b_____n

Write the Spelling Words below.

_____   _____

_____   _____

_____   _____

_____   _____

_____   _____

_____   _____

Spelling Words

1. of
2. do
3. to
4. what
5. write
6. myself
7. name
8. time
9. went
10. been
11. too
12. little

Theme 3: **Neighborhood and Community**   155

Name _____

Spelling Spree

Choose a Spelling Word to complete each sentence. Write the words in the puzzles.

1. My _____ is Alex.
2. It is _____ for school.
3. My brother wants to go _____.
4. What will he _____?
5. He is too _____.
6. I will _____ a note.
7. I will ask if he can come _____ school.
8. He can come at the end _____ the day.

Write the Spelling Word that is made up of two little words.

9. _____

Write the Spelling Word that can ask a question.

10. _____

Name _____

Proofreading and Writing

Proofreading Find and circle misspelled Spelling Words below. Then write each word correctly.

October 5, 2001

Dear Akimi,

It has not ben a good day. I whent to a new school. I did not know anyone in my class. I did not know whut to answer when the teacher asked me a question. I ate lunch by miself. In the afternoon I had to rite a story about my day.

Your friend,
Benita

Spelling Words

1. of
2. do
3. to
4. what
5. write
6. myself
7. name
8. time
9. went
10. been
11. too
12. little

1. _____   4. _____

2. _____   5. _____

3. _____

✏️ **Write and Draw a Community Poster** On construction paper, write the name of a community helper. Then write sentences that tell how that person helps. Use as many Spelling Words as you can.

Name _____

Train Play

Write the word that goes with each sentence.

Word Bank

| train | wait | play | stay | day | paid |

1. Our class went to visit a fire station one _____.

2. We had to ride a _____ to get there.

3. The teacher _____ for our tickets.

4. We did not have to _____ for the train.

5. We had to _____ together when we walked.

6. We knew we could not _____ while the firefighters showed us around.

Now write each word under the train that has the same vowel pair.

pail

may

_____   _____

_____   _____

_____   _____

Name _____

Compound Word Find

**Underline the compound words in the letter. Then
add three sentences. Use words in the box to make
compound words. Use those words in your sentences.**

Word Bank

| day | dash | body | light | some | every |

Dear Grandmother,

   Our new neighbor is a firefighter. Her

name is Ms. Sanchez.

   She let me visit the fire station yesterday.

I took my notebook so I could take lots of notes.

Ms. Sanchez showed me the water truck, the

ambulance, and the ladder truck. They park the

trucks in the firehouse driveway.

_____

_____

_____

Name _____

Word Clues

Write a word from the box to complete the sentences.

Word Bank

clothes	guess	order

Find out what job Cal wants to do when he grows up. Read the clues to find out. Write the answer on the last line.

1. He wants to help people.

2. He will wear _____ that keep him safe from a fire. He will wear a big helmet, rubber boots, and a heavy coat.

3. He will drive a big truck.

4. He will help keep the buttons, knobs, and water hoses on his truck in working _____.

   Can you _____ what job Cal wants to do? _____

Name _____

Firefighter Words

Write a word or words from the box to tell what each sentence describes.

Vocabulary

chief	gear	emergencies
firefighters	dispatch	fire engine

1. I am a truck with a siren and lights.

   _____

2. I tell the people what to do. _____

3. Air tanks and an ax can be very

   helpful. _____

4. We race to the fire and put it out.

   _____

5. Fires are burning and people need help.

   _____

6. When a message arrives, help is soon on

   the way. _____

Name _____

Firehouse Chart

Complete the chart below as you read the story.

Topic

A Trip to the Firehouse

FIRE DEPARTMENT

Main Idea

The firefighters show the

children many exciting things.

Detail _____

Detail _____

Detail _____

Detail _____

Detail _____

Name _____

A Firefighter Is Talking

Write your answers on the lines.

Pretend you are a firefighter. You are being asked questions on a TV show.

What kind of gear do firefighters wear?

1._____

_____

_____

Why is there a pole in a firehouse?

2._____

_____

_____

What happens in the dispatch room in a firehouse?

3._____

_____

_____

Why is it important to make sure all the equipment works?

4._____

_____

_____

Name _____

What's the Idea?

Read the newspaper story.

House Catches Fire

There was a fire in the kitchen of the Reese family home Thursday morning. The house is at 4301 Oak Line Drive. Two neighbors saw thick smoke coming through a window. One neighbor ran to her house to call 911. She told the emergency operator where the fire was. Another neighbor ran to the Reese house. She helped everyone in the family get out of the house safely.

The emergency operator called the fire station. A water truck and a fire engine were dispatched. The firefighters got to the Reese house within ten minutes. The firefighters hooked long hoses up to the water truck. They aimed the water at the fire. Soon, the fire was out. Everyone was safe because of the neighbors and the work of the firefighters.

The Reese family was happy that no one was hurt. The Reese family thanked the firefighters. They also thanked their neighbors.

Name _____

What's the Idea? continued

Use the newspaper story about the fire at the Reese home to complete the chart below.

Topic: _____

Main Idea: _____

_____

Detail 1: _____

_____

Detail 2: _____

_____

Detail 3: _____

_____

Detail 4: _____

_____

Name _____

Consonant Choice

Write the word that completes each sentence.

1. Clang! Clang! The fire engine

   _____ down the street.

showed   rushed

2. The firefighters wanted to

   _____ the fire in a hurry.

reach   chain

3. The fire engine stopped at a plant

   _____.

ship   shop

4. There was a fire burning in a

   _____.

wheelbarrow   whale

5. Many people stopped to _____
   the firefighters work.

watch   check

6. _____ quickly pulled out
   the water hoses.

Those   They

7. The firefighters sprayed water

   _____.

when   everywhere

8. The store owner _____ the
   firefighters before they left.

thought   thanked

Name _____

ai or ay?

Most of the words have the long **a** sound
spelled **ay** or **ai**.

    the long **a** sound ⟶ **way, train**

▶ The word **they** is special. The vowels **ey**
spell the long **a** sound in **they**.

▶ The word **great** is special. The vowels
ea spell the long **a** sound in **great**.

**Write each Spelling Word under the hat with the
matching letters.**

_____   _____

_____   _____

_____   _____

_____

Write the special words that have a star next to them.

_____   _____

Spelling Words
1. train
2. way
3. mail
4. play
5. trail
6. pay
7. sail
8. hay
9. nail
10. rain
11. they*
12. great*

Name _____

Spelling Spree

Maze Play Connect the words with the long *a*
sound to help the fire truck get to the fire.

1. train
2. way
3. mail
4. play
5. trail
6. pay
7. sail
8. hay
9. nail
10. rain
11. they*
12. great*

cat   nail   back

hay   pan   pay

ball   train

mail   cab

dad   trail

way   ant

sail

Write each Spelling Word in the maze under its long *a* sound.

ai   ay

1. _____   6. _____

2. _____   7. _____

3. _____   8. _____

4. _____

5. _____

Name _____

Proofreading and Writing

Proofreading **Circle the four Spelling Words that are wrong in this letter. Then write each word correctly.**

Dear Chief Rogers,   January 23, 2001

We had a grate time at the fire station! It was fun to pla with Spot, the firehouse dog. Everyone liked washing the fire truck too. The way the water came out of the hose looked like ran. I liked watching the firefighters get ready to go fight a fire. Thay dressed really fast. May I come visit another day?

Sincerely,
Tony

Spelling Words

1. train
2. way
3. mail
4. play
5. trail
6. pay
7. sail
8. hay
9. nail
10. rain
11. they*
12. great*

_____   _____

_____   _____

Write What You Want to See
What would you like to see if you could visit a firehouse? Write it on a separate sheet of paper. Use Spelling Words from the list.

Name _____

Dictionary Word Match

Read the word list. Write each word under the place where you would find it in the dictionary. Would the word be found in the beginning, middle, or end?

Beginning
A–K

Middle
L–S

End
T–Z

_____   _____   _____

_____   _____   _____

_____   _____   _____

_____

Name _____

Names of Nouns

► A special noun is a word that names a certain, or special, person, place, or thing.

► A special noun always begins with a capital letter.

Read each noun below. Write a special noun for it. Choose special nouns from the box.

Word Bank

Red River

Mrs. Carlos

Texas

Spot

Bay City

Playland Park

Golden Gate
  Bridge

Mr. Davis

1. park _____

2. woman _____

3. bridge _____

4. dog _____

5. state _____

6. river _____

7. city _____

8. man _____

Write two sentences about a place you like to visit. Use a special noun in each sentence.

_____

_____

_____

Name _____

Name Those Facts

► A special noun is a word that names a certain, or special, person, place, or thing.
► A special noun always begins with a capital letter.

special person   special place   special thing

Complete each sentence with a special noun that tells about you.

 1. My name is _____.

 2. My street address is _____.

 3. The name of my teacher is _____.

 4. My favorite place to eat is _____.

 5. My favorite story is called _____.

Name _____

Special Names

**Replace the words in dark print with special names.
Write the names on the lines below.**

May 29, 2001

Dear Joan,

    Today was a very exciting **day**. **My friend** and I were walking down **the street**. A fire truck came racing past us. It stopped at the house of **our neighbor**. We ran to see what was wrong. We found that **a cat** was stuck in a tree.

Yours truly,

Meg

1. _____

2. _____

3. _____

4. _____

5. _____

**On the lines below, write a sentence about a
friend. Use a special name in your sentence.**

6. _____

_____

Name _____

Web Notes

Read the paragraph. Write your notes about the paragraph in the web.

Fire Safety Rules

Suppose you are in a building that catches fire. First stay calm. Warn everyone in the building about the fire. Be careful though, you must get out quickly. Feel doors to see if they are hot. If they are, the fire may be burning on the other side. See if there is another way out. Once you are out, call the firefighters. Never go back inside a burning building.

Detail

Detail

Topic

Detail

Detail

Name _____

Making It Clear

Read the dialogue. Then rewrite the Caller's answers.
Add special nouns that give exact information.

Emergency Operator: 911 Operator.
Caller: There is a fire at a store.

_____

_____

Emergency Operator: What is the address?
Caller: The store is near a busy street.

_____

_____

Emergency Operator: What is your name?
Caller: Pam.

_____

_____

Emergency Operator: Where are you now?
Caller: I'm looking out the window of a house.

_____

_____

Emergency Operator: Stay where you are. Help
will be there in a few minutes.

Name _____

Letter Magic

Change one letter in each word in dark print to
make a new word that will finish each sentence.
Each new word should have the letters
ow **or** *ou* **in it.**

1. **cut**   He's not going in. He's going _____ .

2. **cot**   That's not a pig. That's a _____ .

3. **load**   She's not being quiet. She's being _____ .

4. **horse**   That's not a barn. That's a _____ .

5. **flowed**   That's not a tree. That's a _____ .

6. **short**   Speak softly. Don't _____ .

Look at the words you wrote. Choose one word that
has the letters *ou* **and one word that has the letters** *ow***.**
Write a sentence with each of those words.

7. _____

8. _____

Name _____

Suffix Fun

Write the base word of each underlined word.

1. Sarah likes her <u>colorful</u> costume. _____

2. She feels <u>playful</u> when she puts it on. _____

3. On the stage, she has to sing <u>loudly</u>. _____

4. But at home she sings <u>quietly</u> to herself. _____

5. She had to learn her songs <u>quickly</u>. _____

6. She thinks she has a <u>wonderful</u> part in the play.

_____

Add *-ly* or *-ful* to the words below to make new words.

7. friend _____

8. thought _____

9. hope _____

10. most _____

Name _____

Use the Words

Word Bank

behind   soldier   story

Answer each riddle with a word from the box.

1. I have a beginning and an end. What am I? _____

2. I keep our country safe. Who am I? _____

3. I mean the opposite of "in front." _____

Write a short story about a soldier who sees a horse behind a tree. Use all of the words from the box in your story.

_____

_____

_____

_____

Name _____

Costume Play

José is in the school play. Follow these directions to show how José will look.

Directions:

1. Draw the costume of a king on José. Include a crown.
2. Draw a bushy beard.
3. Draw a big mustache.

José and his mom are talking. Use the words in the box to complete their sentences.

> **Vocabulary**
>
> handsome   disguise   mirror

Mom: "What a _____ king we have here!"

José: "I'm not really a king. I'm wearing a _____."

Mom: "Then who are you?"

José: "I'm José, your son."

Mom: "You'd better look in a _____ to be sure!"

Name _____

Problem-Solving Event Map

As you read the story, complete the Problem-Solving Event Map below.

Problem: Ricky loses the _____ his teacher gave him.

What Ricky Tries	Predict: Will this solve the problem?		Check
_____	Yes	No	_____
_____	Yes	No	_____
_____	Yes	No	_____
_____	Yes	No	_____
_____	Yes	No	_____
_____	Yes	No	_____
_____	Yes	No	_____

Name _____

True or Not True?

Print the word *True* or *Not true* after each sentence.

1. Ricky was happy that he looked like his mother. _____

2. Mrs. Cortez asked the children to leave their

    costumes in their desks. _____

3. Ricky looked older with his mustache on. _____

4. Ricky told his father all about the lost mustache. _____

5. Ricky tried to make his own mustache. _____

6. Ricky's father shaved his mustache so he would

    look more like Ricky. _____

7. Ricky's new mustache was a special gift from

    his father. _____

**Find each sentence that was *Not true*. On the lines
below, rewrite each sentence to make it true.**

8. _____

9. _____

   _____

10. _____

   _____

Theme 3: **Neighborhood and Community**   **181**

Problem-Solving

Read the story. Then complete the chart on the next page.

The Cookie Problem

Mike's class wanted to do something special for the children at the hospital. They decided to raise money to buy books. They would have a cookie sale at school. Everyone would bring cookies to sell.

When he got home, Mike asked his mother for help making cookies. She reminded him that she had to go to work soon.

Mike asked his father for help. His father wanted to help, but he had promised to help Mike's sister build her science project.

Mike decided to count his money. He had been saving to buy a new model to build. He could buy cookies, but then he would have to wait even longer to get the model.

Then Mike had an idea. He called his friend Tran. They could make cookies together! Tran's grandfather would help them. Mike took sugar and flour to Tran's house. Mike and Tran and Tran's grandfather made cookies. The next day, the class sold cookies. They used the money to buy ten books for the children at the hospital.

Name _____

Problem-Solving continued

After you've read the story "The Cookie Problem," answer this question.

What is Mike's problem?

_____

In the box on the left, write each solution Mike tries. In the box on the right, write why it doesn't work.

Solution

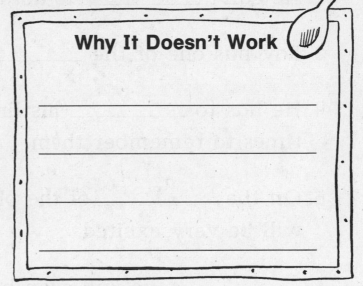

Why It Doesn't Work

Mike's last solution does work. Write the solution and why it works.

_____

_____

Do you think Mike's solution is a good one? Why or why not?

_____

Name _____

Play Day

Choose the word with *ai* or *ay* that correctly completes each sentence. Write the word on the line.

1. Ray has a part in the school _____ . | play   jail |

2. He can't _____ to act on the stage. | stay   wait |

3. Ray has one of the _____ parts. | main   hay |

4. He has to _____ his lines many times to remember them. | main   say |

5. On the _____ of the play, Ray will be very excited. | day   main |

6. _____ he will even be the star of the play! | faintly   maybe |

Write two sentences of your own. Use an *ai* word in one sentence and an *ay* word in the other.

_____

_____

Name _____

The Vowel Sound in COW

The words **town** and **house** have the same
vowel sound. This vowel sound may be
spelled **ow** or **ou**.   The words **could** and
should do not follow this rule.

**Write the Spelling Words with the *ow* sound
spelled *ow*.**

flower

1. _____   4. _____

2. _____   5. _____

3. _____   6. _____

**Write the Spelling Words with the *ow* sound
spelled *ou*.**

out

7. _____   9. _____

8. _____   10. _____

Write the Spelling Words that rhyme with *good*.

11. _____   12. _____

Spelling Words

1. town
2. house
3. sour
4. frown
5. cow
6. clown
7. found
8. how
9. mouse
10. brown
11. could*
12. should*

Name _____

Spelling Spree

Spelling Scramble Unscramble the letters to make a Spelling Word.

Spelling Words

1. town
2. house
3. sour
4. frown
5. cow
6. clown
7. found
8. how
9. mouse
10. brown
11. could*
12. should*

1. w n o r f   ___ ___ ___ ___ ___

2. s d u o h l   ___ ___ ___ ___ ___ ___

3. u s o h e   ___ ___ ___ ___ ___

4. w o r n b   ___ ___ ___ ___ ___

5. u o l d c   ___ ___ ___ ___ ___

6. w n l c o   ___ ___ ___ ___ ___

Fill-in Fun Write the missing Spelling Word to create a pair of words that go together.

7. sweet and _____

8. lost and _____

9. _____ and country

10. cat and _____

Name _____

Proofreading and Writing

**Proofreading Circle four Spelling Words that are
spelled wrong in this note. Then write each word
correctly.**

Dear Parents,

    For the school play, could you help us

with costumes? Here's what we need:

▶ A tail for the couw

▶ Big shoes for the cloun

▶ Broun pants and shirt for the mowse

Thank you for your help!

      Mr. Jackson

Spelling Words

1. town
2. house
3. sour
4. frown
5. cow
6. clown
7. found
8. how
9. mouse
10. brown
11. could*
12. should*

1. _____ 3. _____

2. _____ 4. _____

**Write a Letter Pretend you have just been in a play
about Cinco de Mayo. On a separate piece of paper,
write a letter to a friend. Tell about the play. Use
Spelling Words from the list.**

Name _____

Search for Meaning

Read each sentence. Use the context to figure out what the underlined word means. Write the letter for the meaning of the word on the line next to each sentence.

_____ 1. When our team scored the winning point, the fans cheered for our <u>victory</u>.

_____ 2. We <u>celebrated</u> by inviting all of our friends to eat cake and sing.

_____ 3. We <u>rushed</u> home so we could be the first ones there for the party.

_____ 4. Rosie lost her hat, so she <u>retraced</u> her steps and looked everywhere she had been.

_____ 5. My mother's special <u>creation</u> for the party was a drink she made from ice cream, pineapple, and bananas.

Meanings

A. went back over

B. win or getting first place

C. something made up

D. had a party for a special reason

E. went quickly

Name _____

Which Is Which?

▶ Nouns can name one thing or more than one thing.

▶ Most nouns add -s to name more than one.

▶ Nouns that end in **s**, **x**, **ch**, and **sh** add -**es** to name
more than one.

**Look at the nouns in the box. Some name one thing and
some name more than one thing. Write the nouns that name
one thing below the flag. Write the nouns that name more
than one thing below the group of flags.**

Word Bank

boxes	shoes	dishes	dresses	mustache
pocket	apples	wish	fox	father

_____

_____

_____

_____

Name _____

What Do You See?

Remember:

► Nouns can name one thing or more than one thing.

► Most nouns add **-s** to name more than one.

► Nouns that end in **s**, **x**, **ch**, and **sh** add **-es** to name more than one.

Write what you see in each box. The first one has been done for you.

apple

I see two apples

_____.

mustache

I see _____

_____.

dress

I see _____

_____.

six

I see _____

_____.

watch

I see _____

_____.

dish

I see _____

_____.

Where's That Mustache?

Remember:
- ► Nouns can name one thing or more than one thing.
- ► Most nouns add **-s** to name more than one.
- ► Nouns that end in **s**, **x**, **ch**, and **sh** add **-es** to name more than one.

Suppose Ricky wrote a report about his lost mustache.
He made five mistakes in his report. Circle his
mistakes. Then write each word correctly.

I lost my mustache. I looked everywhere for it. I looked in my pocketes. I looked in the boxs in my closet. I looked under the dishs. I looked under the chaires in the kitchen. I even looked under the benchs in the park. Then my mother surprised me with a new mustache!

1. _____   4. _____

2. _____   5. _____

3. _____

Name _____

What Is the Problem?

Think of a problem that you have had. How did
you solve it? What did you learn from the problem
and the solution? Use this chart to help you
organize your ideas about the problem.

1. What was the problem? How did it come up?

_____

_____

2. How did you solve the problem?

_____

_____

3. What did you learn from solving the problem?

_____

_____

Name _____

Solving a Problem

Read the school newspaper report. It tells about a play put on by the second grade. Make the writing more interesting by replacing the underlined words with exact nouns. Write your choices for exact nouns on the lines below.

Last night, the second grade put on a play. The teacher said it was about Cinco de Mayo. Two children played instruments. One girl told the story. All the students wore costumes. Boys wore sombreros and carried things. Girls wore skirts and serapes. When the play ended, everyone clapped.

1. _____

2. _____

3. _____

4. _____

5. _____

Name _____

Rhyme Time

**Here are some poems about painting. Finish each poem.
Write a word from the box that rhymes with the last word in
the first sentence.**

Word Bank

dream	easy	sea	street	week

1. The beach is a place where I like to be.

   That's where I go when I paint the _____.

2. Things are not always what they seem.

   Today I'll paint a funny _____.

3. Here's a painting of a dog with furry feet.

   He's walking down a busy _____.

4. How can I paint on a day that's breezy?

   That's a job that won't be _____!

5. At this painting you may not peek.

   You will have to wait a _____.

Name _____

What Do You See?

Choose a word from the box to label each picture.

Word Bank

celebration   furniture   lotion   nature   picture   vacation

_____   _____

_____   _____

_____   _____

Name _____

I Believe in Art

The Lady with
the Flowers

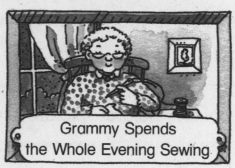

Grammy Spends
the Whole Evening Sewing

I Can't Believe I Ate the
Whole Thing!

Write the name of the painting to answer each question.

1. Which painting shows someone with a needle
   and thread?

   _____

2. Which painting shows someone sitting in front
   of an empty plate?

   _____

3. Which painting shows someone carrying roses?

   _____

Make your own drawing called *I Believe in Happiness*.

I Believe in Happiness

Name _____

Subway Words

Maria is new to the city. She asks her friend Lulu how to get around. Finish the sentences with words from the box.

> ### Vocabulary
>
> booth   plaque   station   subway   token

Maria: How can I get around in the city?

Lulu: You can use the _____.

Maria: Where can I go to find it?

Lulu: You will find a _____ close to your house.

Maria: Then what do I do?

Lulu: You go down the stairs and find a _____ where you buy a _____. Then you get on the train.

Maria: How do I know where to get off?

Lulu: When the train slows down, look out the window. You will see a _____ with the name of the station on it.

Name _____

I Can Use Clues Chart

As you read, use clues from the story to make guesses about what Jamaica and the other people in the story are like. Write your guesses and the clues on the chart.

Story: Jamaica Louise James

What the Character Is Like	Story Clues
_____	_____
_____	_____
_____	_____
_____	_____
_____	_____
_____	_____
_____	_____
_____	_____

Name _____

How Does It Feel?

Read each sentence. Choose the word that best completes the sentence. Write the word on the line.

Word Bank

worried	mad	excited	proud	happy	scared

1. Grammy and Mama are _____ about their birthday present for Jamaica. They want her to open it quickly.

2. Jamaica is _____ about how much the present cost.

3. Grammy is not _____ to work at night, but Jamaica is afraid of the night.

4. The grown-ups in the subway always look so _____.

5. Grammy is very _____ when she sees Jamaica's paintings.

6. Now the people in the subway seem _____. They like Jamaica's presents.

Name _____

Making Inferences

Read the story. Then answer the questions on page 201.

Luann's House

Luann lives with her Aunt Sonya and Uncle Leo on the top floor of their building. Luann's best friend lives next door. Her name is Carla.

Luann has three pets. She has a gerbil in a small cage, a parrot in a big cage, and a cat that likes to go on the roof. Luann gives her gerbil balls of cotton to make into nests. She feeds the parrot pieces of fruit and slices of bread. When Luann and Carla go up to the roof, Luann brings her cat.

Uncle Leo reads in a big chair with a light behind it. Sometimes he reads to Carla and Luann about the new paintings at the museum.

Aunt Sonya has a garden on the roof. She grows roses. She knows the names of all the roses. Sometimes she brings fresh bread and iced tea up to the roof for the girls.

Name _____

Making Inferences continued

Use the things you know about Luann from the story to answer the questions. Do the same with Uncle Leo and Aunt Sonya.

1. What is special about Luann?

   _____

   _____

   _____

Luann

2. What kind of person is Uncle Leo?

   _____

   _____

   _____

Uncle Leo

3. Would you like Aunt Sonya to take care of you for an afternoon? Why?

   _____

   _____

Aunt Sonya

Name _____

Riddle Fun

Find two words from the box that go together to match each description.

Word Bank

clown	cow	growling	frowning
house	mouse	loud	prowling

1. A place where there is lots of noise

_____

2. A small animal sneaking around

_____

3. A funny guy at the circus who is unhappy

_____

4. An angry animal that gives milk

_____

Name _____

E? Ea? Ee?

The vowel sound in **we**, **keep**, and **clean** is the long **e** sound. The long **e** sound may be spelled **e**, **ee**, or **ea**.

► The words **people** and **the** do not follow this pattern.

Write the Spelling Words with the long *e* sound spelled *e*.

_____ _____

Write the Spelling Words with the long *e* sound spelled *ee*.

_____ _____ _____

Write the Spelling Words with the long *e* sound spelled *ea*.

_____ _____

_____ _____

Write the two Spelling Words you have not written.

_____ _____

Spelling Words

1. clean
2. keep
3. please
4. feel
5. we
6. be
7. eat
8. tree
9. mean
10. read
11. the*
12. people*

Name _____

Spelling Spree

Rhyming Clues Write a Spelling Word for each clue.

1. It begins with the letter **e**.

   It rhymes with **feet**. _____

2. It begins with the letters **tr**.

   It rhymes with **me**. _____

3. It begins with the letter **w**.

   It rhymes with **he**. _____

4. It begins with the letter **r**.

   It rhymes with **feed**. _____

5. It begins with the letter **b**.

   It rhymes with **see**. _____

6. It begins with the letters **cl**.

   It rhymes with **bean**. _____

7. It begins with the letter **k**.

   It rhymes with **deep**. _____

8. It begins with the letter **m**.

   It rhymes with **seen**. _____

Name _____

Proofreading and Writing

Proofreading Circle four Spelling Words that are spelled wrong. Then write each word correctly.

New Artist in Town

Many peaple came to see th paintings of Jamaica Louise James yesterday. She paints the things around her. She paints her family, houses, cats, and dogs. One special painting is a picture of a tree. Her paintings make us all feal happy. Pleese don't miss her wonderful show of paintings! The show will be open for one more day.

Spelling Words

1. clean
2. keep
3. please
4. feel
5. we
6. be
7. eat
8. tree
9. mean
10. read
11. the*
12. people*

1. _____   3. _____

2. _____   4. _____

✏️ **Write a Review** On a separate sheet of paper, write about a painting you have seen. Tell what you like about the painting. Use Spelling Words from the list.

Theme 3: **Neighborhood and Community**   205

Name _____

Where to Find It

Word Bank

lake	laugh	drove	dream
drip	lamb	late	drum
law	dry	dress	land

Look at the dictionary guide words below. Write each word from the box on the correct dictionary page.

draw/drive

_____

_____

_____

drop/duck

_____

_____

_____

lake/large

_____

_____

_____

last/lazy

_____

_____

_____

206   Theme 3: **Neighborhood and Community**

Which Word?

**Choose the best word for each
sentence and write it on the line.**

1. Jamaica often plays with

   other _____.

   | child | children |

2. One _____ gave her a
   flower.

   | child | children |

3. Jamaica painted the _____
   with the green hat.

   | woman | women |

4. The four _____ in the subway
   liked her paintings.

   | man | men |

5. One _____ said the paintings
   made her feel happy.

   | woman | women |

6. A _____ who was an artist
   looked at the paintings.

   | man | men |

7. One _____ gave Jamaica
   a big hug.

   | woman | women |

8. The _____ at Jamaica's school
   went to see her paintings.

   | child | children |

Name _____

One or More Than One

Write the word that goes with each drawing.

Word Bank

| men | mice | woman | mouse |
| teeth | man | tooth | women |

1. _____

2. _____

3. _____

4. _____

5. _____

6. _____

7. _____

8. _____

Name _____

What's the Plural?

**Circle the five words that are not correct. Then write
each word correctly.**

March 3, 2001

    Today I saw three womans wearing big

hats. The hats had bright yellow flowers on

them. I saw two childs playing in the park.

They had pet mouses that crawled up their

arms. I wonder if a mouse has sharp tooths.

Then I saw four mans carrying a piano. Their

faces were red.

1. _____

2. _____

3. _____

4. _____

5. _____

Theme 3: **Neighborhood and Community**   209

Name _____

Get Ready to Write Your Ad

**Use this form to help you write your ad. Remember
that you are trying to convince someone to buy
your product. Think about who might buy it and
what you could say to convince them to buy it.**

James Advertising Agency

Name of what I'm going to sell: _____

Who will buy it? _____

Tell about the person who will buy it. _____

_____

_____

Tell why your product is special. _____

_____

Name two reasons why someone should buy it.

_____

_____

Name _____

Who Will Use It?

Here are three items for sale. On each line, write who
might buy the item. Then read what the ad might say.
Circle the best phrase for each ad.

Who will use it?

_____

> Easy to Use!
>
> Dries in 2 Days
>
> Child-proof Bottle

Who will use it?

_____

> Smells Like Bubble Gum!
>
> Makes Shaving Easy!
>
> Great for Art Projects!

Who will use it?

_____

> Fresh Smell of Hay!
>
> Smell Like a Rose Garden!
>
> Attracts Bees Like Daisies Do!

Name _____

Writing a Personal Response

Use the test-taking strategies and tips you have learned to help you answer questions that ask what you think about something. Then read your answer and see how you may make it better. This practice will help you when you take this kind of test.

Choose one idea to write about. Write at least one paragraph about your topic.

a. How do you know that the boy and his grandmother enjoy being together in the story **Chinatown**? Whom in your family do you like spending time with? What do you do together?

b. Why do you think the New Year's celebration is important to the boy and his grandmother? Tell about a celebration that is important to you. What is the celebration? Why is it important to you?

_____

_____

_____

_____

Writing a Personal Response

continued

Read your answer. Check to be sure that it

- sticks to the topic
- is well organized
- has details that support your answer
- has describing and exact words
- has few mistakes in capitalization, punctuation, grammar,
  or spelling

Now pick one way you can make your answer better.
Make your changes below.

_____

_____

_____

_____

_____

_____

_____

_____

Name _____

Spelling Review

Write Spelling Words to answer the questions.

1–8. Which words are spelled with **th, wh, sh,** or **ch**?

1. _____   5. _____

2. _____   6. _____

3. _____   7. _____

4. _____   8. _____

9–17. Which words that you haven't written have the long **a** or long **e** sound?

9. _____   14. _____

10. _____   15. _____

11. _____   16. _____

12. _____   17. _____

13. _____

18–20. Which words have the vowel sound in **cow**?

18. _____   19. _____   20. _____

Spelling Words

1. tray
2. when
3. teeth
4. than
5. be
6. eat
7. sheep
8. play
9. frown
10. sail
11. chase
12. teach
13. please
14. train
15. wash
16. which
17. found
18. we
19. tree
20. mouse

Name _____

Around Town:
Neighborhood and
Community: Theme 3
Wrap-Up

Spelling Review

Spelling Spree

Hidden Words Circle the Spelling Word hidden in each group of letters below. Write the word on the line.

1. lpmouseto _____

2. qtreemba _____

3. arlfrownp _____

4. vgiwhich _____

5. fsheepmse _____

1. frown
2. teach
3. tree
4. sheep
5. which
6. mouse
7. we
8. play
9. sail
10. found

Rhyming Clues Write a Spelling Word for each clue.

6. It rhymes with **round**.
   It begins like **fan**. _____

7. It rhymes with **beach**.
   It begins like **table**. _____

8. It rhymes with **gray**.
   It begins like **plate**. _____

9. It rhymes with **be**.
   It begins like **worm**. _____

10. It rhymes with **mail**.
    It begins like **sun**. _____

Name _____

Proofreading and Writing

Proofreading Circle four Spelling Words that are wrong. Then write each word correctly.

> Come to a block party! It will bea this Friday. Come enjoy good things to eet. Bring the whole family, plese!
>
> The party starts at five P.M. It will end wen you want to go home!

Spelling Words

1. chase
2. when
3. train
4. than
5. please
6. teeth
7. be
8. wash
9. tray
10. eat

1. _____   3. _____

2. _____   4. _____

A Party Plan Write Spelling Words to complete this plan.

Dad, take the early 5._____ home. Mom, 6._____ the vegetables for the party and put them on a 7._____. Maya, don't let the dog 8._____ the cat! T.J., brush your 9._____. We'll have more fun 10._____ we've ever had!

Write a Diary Entry Write a diary entry about the block party. Use another sheet of paper. Use the Spelling Review Words.

My Handbook

Contents

Trace and write the letters.

Aa Aa

Bb Bb

Cc Cc

Dd Dd

Ee Ee

Ff Ff

Gg Gg

Trace and write the letters.

Hh Hh

Ii Ii

Jj Jj

Kk Kk

Ll Ll

Mm Mm

Trace and write the letters.

Nn Nn

Oo Oo

Pp Pp

Qq Qq

Rr Rr

Ss Ss

Tt Tt

Trace and write the letters.

Uu Uu

Vv Vv

Ww Ww

Xx Xx

Yy Yy

Zz Zz

Trace and write the letters.

Aa Aa

Bb Bb

Cc Cc

Dd Dd

Ee Ee

Ff Ff

Gg Gg

Trace and write the letters.

 Hh Hh

 Ii Ii

Jj Jj

Kk Kk

Ll Ll

 Mm Mm

Trace and write the letters.

Nn Nn

Oo Oo

Pp Pp

Qq Qq

Rr Rr

Ss Ss

Tt Tt

Trace and write the letters.

Uu Uu

Vv Vv

Ww Ww

Xx Xx

Yy Yy

Zz Zz

Silly Stories:
Reading-Writing Workshop

Look carefully at how these words are spelled.

Spelling Words

1. the	7. it
2. will	8. they
3. have	9. as
4. was	10. my
5. you	11. off
6. said	12. any

Challenge Words

1. because
2. family

My Study List
Add your own spelling words on the back. ➡

Dragon Gets By

The Short *a* and Short *i* Sounds

short **a** sound ➡ **am**
　　　　　　　　　 b**a**g
short **i** sound ➡ **is**
　　　　　　　　　 d**i**g

Spelling Words

1. bag	7. ran
2. win	8. if
3. is	9. dig
4. am	10. sat
5. his	11. was
6. has	12. I

Challenge Words

1. scratch
2. picnic

My Study List
Add your own spelling words on the back. ➡

Name_____

 My Study List

1. _____
2. _____
3. _____
4. _____
5. _____
6. _____
7. _____
8. _____
9. _____
0. _____

Review Words

. big

an

How to Study a Word

Lo **k** at the word.
Sa **y** he word.
Thi **k** about the word.
Wri **e** he word.
Che **k** the spelling.

Name_____

 My Study List

1. _____
2. _____
3. _____
4. _____
5. _____
6. _____
7. _____
8. _____
9. _____
10. _____

How to Study a Word

Look at the word.
Say the word.
Think about the word.
Write the word.
Check the spelling.

Mrs. Brown Went to Town

Vowel-Consonant-*e* Spellings

long **a** sound ➡ **late**

long **i** sound ➡ **bite**

Spelling Words

1. bite	7. fine
2. late	8. same
3. size	9. hide
4. made	10. line
5. side	11. give
6. ate	12. have

Challenge Words

1. shake
2. write

My Study List
Add your own spelling words on the back. ➡

Julius

The Short *e, o,* and *u* Sounds

short **e** sound ➡ **we**t, **le**g

short **o** sound ➡ **jo**b, **mo**p

short **u** sound ➡ **nu**t, **fu**n

Spelling Words

1. fox	7. went
2. wet	8. mop
3. nut	9. hug
4. job	10. from
5. leg	11. any
6. fun	12. of

Challenge Words

1. block
2. every

My Study List
Add your own spelling words on the back. ➡

Take-Home Word List

Name_____

 My Study List

1. _____
2. _____
3. _____
4. _____
5. _____
6. _____
7. _____
8. _____
9. _____
10. _____

Review Words

1. red
2. up

How to Study a Word

Look at the word.
Say the word.
Think about the word.
Write the word.
Check the spelling.

Take-Home Word List

Name_____

 My Study List

1. _____
2. _____
3. _____
4. _____
5. _____
6. _____
7. _____
8. _____
9. _____
10. _____

Review Words

1. gate
2. bike

How to Study a Word

Look at the word.
Say the word.
Think about the word.
Write the word.
Check the spelling.

Henry and Mudge and the Starry Night

More Vowel-Consonant-*e* Spellings

long **e** → th**ese**

long **o** → b**one**

long **u** → **use**

Spelling Words

1. bone
2. robe
3. use
4. these
5. rope
6. note
7. cute
8. close
9. hope
10. those
11. one
12. goes

Challenge Words

1. drove
2. mule

My Study List
Add your own spelling words on the back. →

Silly Stories
Spelling Review

Spelling Words

1. am
2. dig
3. fox
4. nut
5. leg
6. hide
7. late
8. ran
9. job
10. fun
11. wet
12. bite
13. made
14. ate
15. sat
16. mop
17. hug
18. went
19. size
20. his

Challenge Words

1. scratch
2. block
3. every
4. shake
5. write

My Study List
Add your own spelling words on the back. →

Take-Home Word List

Name_____

 My Study List

1. _____
2. _____
3. _____
4. _____
5. _____
6. _____
7. _____
8. _____
9. _____
10. _____

How to Study a Word

Look at the word.
Say the word.
Think about the word.
Write the word.
Check the spelling.

Take-Home Word List

Name_____

 My Study List

1. _____
2. _____
3. _____
4. _____
5. _____
6. _____
7. _____
8. _____
9. _____
10. _____

Review Words

1. home
2. nose

How to Study a Word

Look at the word.
Say the word.
Think about the word.
Write the word.
Check the spelling.

Exploring Parks with
Ranger Dockett

Words with Consonant Clusters
t**r**ip, **sw**im, **st**ep, **cl**ub,
ne**xt**, **br**ave, **gl**ad

Spelling Words

1. trip
2. swim
3. step
4. nest
5. club
6. stone
7. next
8. brave
9. glad
10. lost

Challenge Words

1. space
2. storm

My Study List
Add your own
spelling words
on the back. ➡

Nature Walk
Reading-Writing Workshop

**Look carefully at how these
words are spelled.**

Spelling Words

1. on
2. am
3. if
4. from
5. his
6. her
7. come
8. want
9. does
10. goes
11. their
12. there

Challenge Words

1. really
2. caught

My Study List
Add your own
spelling words
on the back. ➡

Take-Home Word List

Name_____

 My Study List

1._____

2._____

3._____

4._____

5._____

6._____

7._____

8._____

9._____

10._____

How to Study a Word

Look at the word.
Say the word.
Think about the word.
Write the word.
Check the spelling.

Take-Home Word List

Name_____

 My Study List

1._____

2._____

3._____

4._____

5._____

6._____

7._____

8._____

9._____

10._____

Review Words

1. frog
2. slip

How to Study a Word

Look at the word.
Say the word.
Think about the word.
Write the word.
Check the spelling.

Nature Walk
Spelling Review

Spelling Words

1. these	11. add
2. use	12. mess
3. swim	13. egg
4. glad	14. hope
5. club	15. trip
6. all	16. stone
7. bone	17. lost
8. cute	18. off
9. next	19. grass
10. brave	20. hill

Challenge Words

1. drove
2. mule
3. space
4. storm
5. across

My Study List
Add your own spelling words on the back. →

Around the Pond:
Who's Been Here?

Words with Double Consonants

be**ll**, o**ff**, me**ss**, a**dd**, e**gg**

Spelling Words

1. bell	6. hill
2. off	7. well
3. all	8. egg
4. mess	9. will
5. add	10. grass

Challenge Words

1. across
2. skill

My Study List
Add your own spelling words on the back. →

Take-Home Word List

Name_____

 My Study List

1._____
2._____
3._____
4._____
5._____
6._____
7._____
8._____
9._____
10._____

Review Words

1. shell
2. kiss

How to Study a Word

Look at the word.
Say the word.
Think about the word.
Write the word.
Check the spelling.

240

Take-Home Word List

Name_____

 My Study List

1._____
2._____
3._____
4._____
5._____
6._____
7._____
8._____
9._____
10._____

How to Study a Word

Look at the word.
Say the word.
Think about the word.
Write the word.
Check the spelling.

240

Around Town:

Neighborhood and Community

Reading-Writing Workshop

Look carefully at how these words are spelled.

Spelling Words

1. write
2. of
3. do
4. to
5. time
6. went
7. myself
8. what
9. name
10. too
11. little
12. been

Challenge Words

1. right
2. thought

My Study List
Add your own spelling words on the back. ➡

Chinatown

Words Spelled with *th, wh, sh,* or *ch*

the **th** sound ➡ **th**en, tee**th**

the **wh** sound ➡ **wh**en

the **sh** sound ➡ **sh**eep, di**sh**

the **ch** sound ➡ **ch**ase, tea**ch**

Spelling Words

1. when
2. sheep
3. both
4. then
5. chase
6. teeth
7. teach
8. dish
9. which
10. than
11. wash
12. catch

Challenge Words

1. lunch
2. whistle

My Study List
Add your own spelling words on the back. ➡

Take-Home Word List

Name_____

 My Study List

1. _____
2. _____
3. _____
4. _____
5. _____
6. _____
7. _____
8. _____
9. _____
10. _____

Review Words

1. she
2. bath

How to Study a Word

Look at the word.
Say the word.
Think about the word.
Write the word.
Check the spelling.

242

Take-Home Word List

Name_____

 My Study List

1. _____
2. _____
3. _____
4. _____
5. _____
6. _____
7. _____
8. _____
9. _____
10. _____

How to Study a Word

Look at the word.
Say the word.
Think about the word.
Write the word.
Check the spelling.

242

Big Bushy Mustache

The Vowel Sound in *cow*

ow ➧ t**ow**n

ou ➧ h**ou**se

Spelling Words

1. town
2. house
3. sour
4. frown
5. cow
6. clown
7. found
8. how
9. mouse
10. brown
11. could
12. should

Challenge Words

1. around
2. towel

My Study List
Add your own
spelling words
on the back. ➧

243

A Trip to the Firehouse

More Long *a* Spellings

long **a** sound ➧ tr**ay**

tr**ai**n

Spelling Words

1. train
2. tray
3. mail
4. play
5. trail
6. pay
7. sail
8. hay
9. nail
10. rain
11. they
12. great

Challenge Words

1. snail
2. subway

My Study List
Add your own
spelling words
on the back. ➧

243

Take-Home Word List

Name_____

 My Study List

1. _____
2. _____
3. _____
4. _____
5. _____
6. _____
7. _____
8. _____
9. _____
10. _____

Review Words

1. stay
2. day

How to Study a Word

Look at the word.
Say the word.
Think about the word.
Write the word.
Check the spelling.

244

Take-Home Word List

Name_____

 My Study List

1. _____
2. _____
3. _____
4. _____
5. _____
6. _____
7. _____
8. _____
9. _____
10. _____

Review Words

1. out
2. now

How to Study a Word

Look at the word.
Say the word.
Think about the word.
Write the word.
Check the spelling.

244

Around Town:

Neighborhood and Community Spelling Review

Spelling Words

1. which	11. sail
2. teach	12. found
3. wash	13. be
4. tray	14. tree
5. frown	15. chase
6. we	16. than
7. eat	17. play
8. when	18. train
9. teeth	19. mouse
10. sheep	20. please

Challenge Words

1. lunch
2. whistle
3. snail
4. around
5. steep

My Study List
Add your own spelling words on the back. →

245

Jamaica Louise James

More Long *e* Spellings

long **e** sound → w**e**

k**ee**p

cl**ea**n

Spelling Words

1. clean	7. eat
2. keep	8. tree
3. please	9. mean
4. feel	10. read
5. we	11. the
6. be	12. people

Challenge Words

1. stream
2. steep

My Study List
Add your own spelling words on the back. →

245

Take-Home Word List

Name_____

 My Study List

1. _____
2. _____
3. _____
4. _____
5. _____
6. _____
7. _____
8. _____
9. _____
10. _____

Review Words

1. he
2. see

How to Study a Word

Look at the word.
Say the word.
Think about the word.
Write the word.
Check the spelling.

Take-Home Word List

Name_____

 My Study List

1. _____
2. _____
3. _____
4. _____
5. _____
6. _____
7. _____
8. _____
9. _____
10. _____

How to Study a Word

Look at the word.
Say the word.
Think about the word.
Write the word.
Check the spelling.